HOW TO BE REALLY INTERESTING

Steve Davis is the world number one snooker player and also a celebrated hard living hellraiser. Seldom out of the gossip pages his previous books have included *The Essential Guide to Romford, Alone in My Hush Puppies* and *101 Things to do with Bob Wilson*, all of them bestsellers.

Steve lives in a small bungalow just outside Romford with his live-in parents, and describes his interests as collecting airline menu cards and tidying out his sock drawer.

Penguin Books

PENGUIN BOOKS

Published by the Penguin Group
27 Wrights Lane, London W8 5TZ, England
Viking Penguin Inc., 40 West 23rd Street, New York, New York 10010, USA
Penguin Books Australia Ltd, Ringwood, Victoria, Australia
Penguin Books Canada Ltd, 2801 John Street, Markham, Ontario, Canada L3R 1B4
Penguin Books (NZ) Ltd, 182-190 Wairau Road, Auckland 10, New Zealand

Penguin Books Ltd, Registered Offices: Harmondsworth, Middlesex, England

Published in Penguin Books 1988

Designed by Paul Elmes and Matthew Evans
at Shape of Things

Photographs by Brian Moody

Filmset in folio light by Creative Text, London.

Printed and bound in Great Britain by Severn Valley Press

CONTENTS

AN INTRODUCTION BY STEVE 'INTERESTING' DAVIS

Hi, welcome to my book.
You know, when I was approached to do a book about my ten years in the game I couldn't think what to write about. Then the idea hit me! Why not write about the one thing I know something about: being interesting!

And that's what you get here. A wild, zany, devil-may-care guide to being interesting.

Call me mad, call me impulsive, but I've put down everything I know about the interesting side of life. It's all here. I lift the lid on Barry and me. I tell you the secrets of the other players. And I take you behind the scenes for a crazy, outrageous look backstage at a Magma concert. And you can't get much more interesting than that.

Convinced you'll never be interesting? Don't despair. I used to feel the same way, but look at me now. And who knows, if you follow the advice in this book you too could finish up as interesting as Romford's most famous son!

Best of luck.

SD

CHAPTER 1

ABOUT ME

Here's where I really shoot the white-water rapids with my thirteen-colour biro as I tell you all about me! I let you know what it's really like to be known as 'Interesting' and the pressures that wearing a mantle like that round your neck day in and day out can bring. Plus a lot more outrageous secrets as well.

Of course it's flattering to be called 'Interesting', and I would never want to change, but it can put you under a lot of strain. After all, being interesting isn't interesting all the time.

Sometimes I simply don't feel like being particularly interesting at all, and, though it's hard to believe, I even start to half wish I was just a little bit duller. I just feel like putting on my *'I'm Not Feeling Really Interesting Today'* T-shirt, to let everyone know how I feel, and staying in bed. But I never do because I can't afford to let people down, and besides, I have my high-roller wildfire mad-jinx label to live up to!

Incidentally, I've got quite a few Steve 'Interesting' Davis T-shirts, for when I'm feeling non-interesting but have to make the effort, and I'm thinking of marketing them. Crazy idea, don't you agree!?

INTERESTING PEOPLE DO IT ON THEIR OWN

MY OTHER TEE SHIRT'S A LACOSTE

BORN TO BE INTERESTING

STEVE SAYS . . .
SOFT SCREW THE HALF
BALL RED INTO THE TOP
RIGHT HAND POCKET TO
LEAVE YOURSELF A
THREE QUARTER BALL
POT ON THE BLACK

Soft Machine, My Sort of Music!

You'll know why people rate me as such a hotball when you learn that my favourite group is the progressive rock group Soft Machine. When I was young I used to cut quite a dash at Soft Machine concerts in my Afghan coat and my purple twenty-six-inch flared corduroy trousers and cheesecloth shirt, dancing along in the aisles to the three-hour drum solo.

At home I have a full set of the Softs' albums. Apart from the music, the other really interesting thing about them is their titles. I can't remember them exactly, but working from memory I think they are called:

Soft Machine 1
Soft Machine 2
Soft Machine 3
Soft Machine 4
Soft Machine 5
Soft Machine 6
Soft Machine 7
Soft Machine 8
Soft Machine 9
Soft Machine 10
Soft Machine 12

Me When I'm on Form.

Me When I'm Not Feeling Very Interesting.

With exciting titles like these, you know the record is going to be good even before you've played it. P.S. I know I've missed one out, I'm not sure but I think it was probably Soft Machine 11.

I suppose if you asked me to name my top ten records, then the list of Soft Machine records I've just given you could double up. But as you're starting to discover the crazy devil-may-care guy I am then I bet you won't be surprised by the outrageously zany selection in *'My Top Twelve'* that I list below. No apologies here, these are simply the best records around. Check them out if you don't believe me. I'll be amazed if you disagree.

My Top Ten

The theme tune to *Ski Sunday*
(with free David Vine poster)
The theme tune to *Ski Sunday* (12″ re-mix)
(with free David Vine poster)
The theme tune to *Question of Sport* (on CD)
(with free David Vine poster)
The Romford Rap
(with free David Vine poster)
Soft Machine 7 (with free David Vine poster)
Snooker Sound Effects 3 (BBC Records)
Snooker Sound Effects 17 (BBC Records)
The *Spitting Image* Chicken Song
Val Doonican Sings the Sex Pistols (bootleg)
Tony Knowles Talks You Through His
147-Maximum (32-record box set)
The Bill Werbenuik Aerobic 12″ (30-second burn mix)
The Best of British Brass (with free Willie Thorn poster)

This is another favourite record from my collection. Some of you may know that one of my really interesting hobbies is 'scratch mix records'. This record helped me enormously when I started to scratch mix myself. It contains hundreds of great sampling scratches. By listening to professional scratches you can improve your own. After a hard day's training there's nothing I like better than to come home, flop in my room, turn the volume on my stereo up full and have a good scratch.

Interesting Productions Present

MAGMA WORLD TOUR 1989

FIFTH FAREWELL TOUR
CONFIRMED DATES

Wilmslow Slipper Baths
Droitwich & District Senior Citizens' Club
The Jubilee Scouts Sports Hall, Prestatyn
The Cosy Kettle Tea Rooms & Grill
Behind the coffee bar, the main bus depot, Haverfordwest
Stockport County Supporters' Club Friday Disco
Steve Davis's garage SOLD OUT
Tunbridge Wells Rotarian Society
The Back Room of the Pig & Whistle, Market Harbour
Oxford Circus Underground Station
Jennifer Jenkinson's Seventh Birthday Party
(plus support Mr Amazing the Balloon Bender)

MAGMA ON TOUR 'EXPERIENCE THE EXPERIENCE'

Pop Promotions

You might get some idea of what an interesting guy I am when I tell you about my step into the world of music promotion. I had previously been approached by Bruce Springsteen to manage his world tour and was considering the offer when out of the blue I received a call from Magma, an obscure French jazz-rock band that no one has ever heard of before (except me). Well, of course, you can imagine which one I chose: Magma. They don't call me Mr Big-Shot Play-for-Broke for nothing. I bet Harvey Goldsmith was quaking in his boots that day when he saw the scoop I'd pulled from under him.

Of course, booking bands and setting up concerts is exactly the same as playing a big game of snooker. Except obviously you don't use a snooker cue when you're booking a band, and you don't actually need a snooker table, or snooker balls ... but apart from that the two things are identical.

Steve Davis, A Very Funny Person

A lot of people have made the mistake of accusing me of not having a sense of humour. This is a mistake. When I'm at the table I have to concentrate totally on my game, and this may make it seem that I am a bit dour and off-putting. Don't be misled. Away from the table I am a regular clown and like nothing better than a good laugh. And to prove the point here is a cartoon that never fails to tickle my ribs!

The player at the table has elected to go for green, even though he can only see half of it and will have to screw down the table into baulk and back again to leave himself on for the loose red over the top pocket. Far better would have been to go for blue, with plenty of lefthand side to run it back up the table and into position for the comparatively simple red behind yellow in the 'D'.

I don't mind telling you I roared for hours when I first saw the joke and I still have a chuckle every time I see it. And I bet you will, too!

Steve Davis has no sense of humour? Don't make me laugh!

GREEN......

EMBASSY WOR!

Snooker Loopy

One of the most memorable days of my life was the time we (the Matchroom Mob) were invited to get together with Chas and Dave (Charles and David) to record our single, *Snooker Loopy*.

Talk about being excited, I could hardly sleep the night before and my neck still tingles when I think back to that fabulous day in the studio with 'the boys', cutting our disc. This was more exciting than any snooker tournament; 'Snooker Loopy nuts are we, me and him and them and me ...' We knew we had a smash hit on our hands the moment we first heard those fantastic lyrics.

Another bonus was being invited to the BBC to perform the song on *Top of the Pops* (one of my favourite TV shows, mainly for sheer naturalness). You can imagine the thrill when I learnt that the guest DJ was Dave Lee Travis. What a treat, I've always been a big fan of DLT's, ever since I heard he was called 'The Hairy Cornflake' (now that's what I call a pretty cheeky nickname), and I was even able to get his autograph and a signed photograph after the show ('To Steve, from DLT [The Hairy Cornflake]'). It was pretty hard getting to sleep that night, I can tell you!

The recording of the Snooker Loopy video. I haven't had so much fun since I discovered individual Kraft cheese slices

Television

I don't get much chance to put my feet up in front of the box, so when I do I like to make it worthwhile.

STEVE'S DEFINITELY WORTH VIDEOING LIST

Anything with Nick Owen in it
Pot Black
The Tennents UK Snooker Championships
The Benson & Hedges Masters
The Embassy World Championships
The World Doubles Championship
A Frame with Davis
Ski Sunday
Sumo

- Programmes for Asian viewers
- *Sporting Triangles* (with Nick Owen)
- Any Party Political Broadcast
- *Midweek Sports Special* (with Nick Owen)
- *Emmerdale Farm* (especially if Nick Owen's in it)
- *John Craven's Newsround* (if hosted by Nick Owen)

CHAPTER 2

HOW TO BE REALLY INTERESTING

WITH A LADY

Being interesting with a lady is one of the most difficult things known to man. The unique reaction that occurs between a man and a woman is often called 'chemistry'. I studied chemistry at school, but never came across this in any lessons I took. But then I was once away for two days with acute milk poisoning, so I suppose I could have missed it then. Mind you, it could have been worse, I could have missed the lesson on potassium permanganate. Now that was really interesting, and I would hate to have missed that!

Too many men fail with women because they simply aren't interesting enough. This chapter is packed full of tips and advice on improving your sexual charisma and shows you how to build up your allure and become even more provocative and appealing than Bob Wilson. One of the tricks with women is to treat them like they are men. This doesn't mean you arrange a piddling contest with them, or sing them the third verse of *Eskimo Nell*. It just means you treat them as equals. I certainly do.

REALLY INTERESTING WOMEN

When Jerry Hall gives you a private number which even Mick doesn't have, then you realize you're playing in the Major League. Yet even Jerry doesn't make it into my list of top ten fab dates, that's how hot the competition is! But here are the ones who did, Steve's female dream ticket!

Wincey Willis
I first fell for Wincey when she was the TV-am weathergirl (and you can't get more romantic than that for a job). Now she's left the weather, but her picture's still got pride of place on my wall.

WPC Phelps from *Crimewatch UK*
Is she the next Marilyn Monroe? The similarities are remarkable. They both are women. And they both took Hollywood by storm, earning them the nickname 'The Blonde Bombshell' (well, except WPC Phelps, she entered the police force).

Judith Chalmers
My most torrid dream is of Judith in a basque and fishnets singing a duet of 'Like a Virgin' with Madonna. Afterwards I get to meet them both and have to choose which one to date. Sorry, Madonna!

Michelle from *EastEnders*
Michelle was married to Lofty, so she's obviously used to a real man. It's a tall order, but I just hope if my chance comes round I can match his standards.

Sue Lawley
You only need to see Sue read the news to know she's a red-hot tiger.

Susan Barlow from *Coronation Street*
When Sue married Mike Baldwin I was devastated. I knew my chance had gone. But then they split, and I had a second chance. Sue may be a bit outrageous for me, but maybe I'm the one to tame her. Plus I'd get Ken Barlow for a father-in-law. Watch this space!

Una Stubbs
Una Stubbs? I only need to hear the name and I go weak. I think Una's one of the most fiercely provocative women I know.

Mrs Nick Owen
Anyone who's married to Mr Incredible himself is bound to get into my dateables list. This is one lady I wouldn't mind getting under my Spiderman duvet cover!!!

A Cautionary Note
I once made the mistake of inviting a girl back to my place for coffee. As we settled down together on the sofa I whispered in her ear that I hadn't really meant coffee when I made the suggestion. She smiled softly and said neither had she. I said what I'd really meant was hot drinking chocolate. At this point she grabbed her coat and stormed off. I won't make the same mistake twice.

WHAT I LOOK FOR IN A WOMAN

Everyone looks for different things in a woman: hair, eyes, figure... but my own first priority is always dental health care. Call me a crazy red-blooded stud if you must, but for me there is no greater turn-on than a high standard of oral hygiene.

Nowadays I always make it very clear what I mean when I invite a girl back, even producing the can of chocolate to show exactly what I've got in mind. I suggest you do likewise to avoid the mistake I made.

On Being Propositioned

Having a famous face means that sometimes you get propositioned by complete strangers. Luckily I have found a simple and effective way out of the problem. I give them Tony Knowles's private number and his price list. Sometimes the propositions can be a bit unnerving. I remember on one occasion I was at the table attempting a difficult brown when a pair of pink frilly ladies' knickers flew across in front of me and landed on the table. On closer inspection I noticed they had a phone number written on them in lipstick. Of course I did what anyone else would do in the circumstances. I quickly made my mind up to go for the pink instead of the brown and played a stun run-round off two cushions to bring the cue ball up the table for the last red.

Talking during Sex

I think it's a great idea to talk during sex (as long as it's about snooker).

Kirk Stevens

Although Kirk has got a 'reputation', he is really very shy with women. I remember once we were both at a disco together, wearing these really cool shades, and there was a girl Kirk fancied over in the corner, but he was too embarrassed to say anything, so I offered to act as matchmaker. I danced over to her and introduced myself and said I liked her trouser suit and did she know that Kirk had got the hots for her. At this point 'she' ripped off my sunglasses and said, 'Steve, stop making a complete fool of yourself or you can find a new manager.' Well, how was I to know it was Barry? I immediately danced back to Kirk and told him what had happened. Kirk said I wasn't to bother as 'she' wasn't his type, and he started to dance with one of the bouncers.

Instant Romance

Here's another handy item to help, the *Instant Romance Scratch-and-Sniff Card*. Scratch the appropriate box before your girlfriend arrives to give the room the ideal scented aura you're looking for. A different scent for each romantic occasion.

Expensive perfume	**Rare orchids**	**Romford**	**Inside of my cue case**
Vick vapour rub	**Marmite/ David Icke**	**Crucible Theatre, Sheffield**	**Smoky bacon crisps**
Len Ganley	**Billingsgate**	**Soft Machine Concert**	**Bill Werbenuik's Hotel Room in the Morning**

Dancing

One of the best ways to impress your date is on the dance floor. Fancy footwork is better than fancy talk any day, and you're listening to someone who is an expert at both. Here's something to help:

THE STEVE DAVIS DISCO DANCE HOME TUTOR

Simply cut out the photographs and staple together in the order indicated. When you flick through the photographs you will see that I appear to 'dance'! Practise at home with this and you too could be scoring in no time.

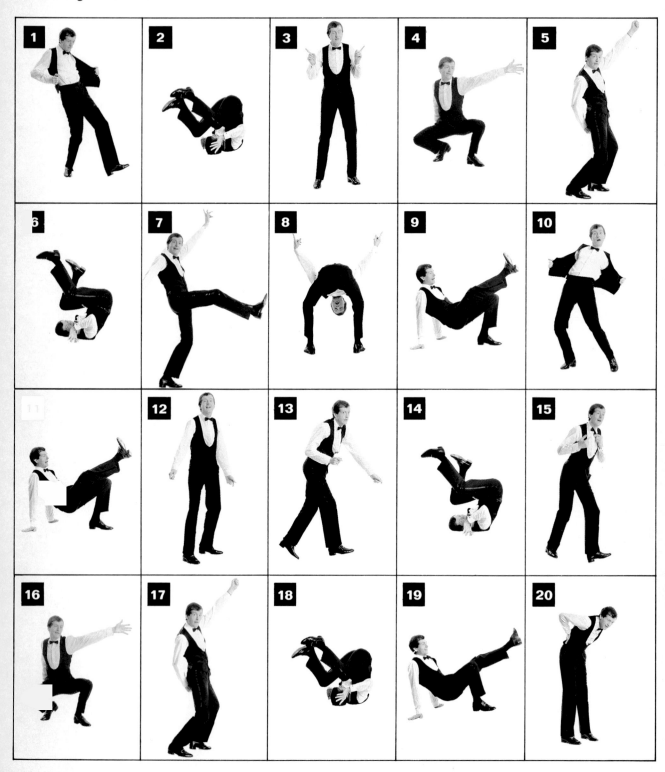

My All-Time Favourite Sure-Fire Chat-Up Lines

'Would you like to hear about my recent break of 137 against Doug Mountjoy?'

'I can probably get two tickets for a Magma concert, if you're interested.'

'Maybe we could go out as a threesome with Clive Everton.'

'Would you like me to get you a glass of milk to put in that whisky, doll?'

'Would you like to come back to my place? I've got a video of last year's Tennents UK final we could watch.'

'Has anyone ever told you you've got snooker player's hands?'

'I scored 26,382 on the space-invaders machine in the local kebab shop last week.'

'I have the largest collection of French jazz-rock records in Essex.'

'Did you read that amazing article in this month's Cue World about the Pirelli Matchroom Fathers and Sons Challenge?'

'What did you say your top break was again?'

'Which do you prefer, Blue Diamonds or Elk Masters?'

'I suppose a frame is out of the question.'

Exciting and Romantic Gifts or You to Give Your Date

Giant Size Snoopy Poster
Giant Size Snoopy Doll
Giant Size Snoopy Address Book
A 'Love Is' staple-gun
A copy of the 1989 *Guinness Book of Snooker Facts and Figures*
A tube of Gibbs New Minty toothpaste
A ten-year subscription to *Snooker Scene*

Aphrodisiacs

As one of the world's greatest lovers, I've often found food can be a powerful aphrodisiac.

- Soup-in-a-Cup
- Cadbury's Smash Instant Mashed Potato
- Boil-in-the-bag meals for one
- 'Mr Men' Yoghurt
- A prawn sandwich in the Matchroom Club (when available)
- A Weetabix and hot milk left to go really mushy
- A 'Funny Feet' ice cream
- A boiled egg and toast dipettes
- A tin of Heinz Meatorites
- A special low-price Berni, only £3.95 on meals taken away before 7.30.
- A packet of cheese and onion crisps and a Bounty
- Big-Mac-Large-Fries-Thick-Shake-Apple-Pie to go

Playing it Cool

There is nothing that turns a girl on more than a guy who is hard to get. Clock these twenty-four-carat-gold hints for success.

- Emigrate to Australia and don't leave a forwarding address.
- When a girl plays footsie with you under the table, lift up your foot and stamp repeatedly on her toe.
- If a girl phones and asks you for a date, say you're not sure and ask if you can phone her back in four years' time. If she phones back in four years' time, tell her to phone you on your private hot line, and give her the following number: (0898) 444 440
- If a girl phones and asks you for a date, ask if your mum can come too.
- Send your girlfriend a valentine card addressed, 'Dear Householder'.
- Start laughing when your girlfriend is kissing you.
- Send your girlfriend flowers at Hallowe'en.
- If you're going out on a blind date, turn up in a full suit of armour.
- Have your name listed in the Yellow Pages under 'Eunuch'.
- Put on forty-five stone and call yourself Bill Werbenuik.

Ten Hints on How to Play Hard to Get

Really Interesting Things a Man and a Woman Can Do Together

- Play Subbuteo
- Have 'His and Hers' face flannels
- Get a larger mortgage
- Share a toothbrush
- Become European Figure-Skating Ice Dance Champions
- Visit each other's parents
- Open a TSB joint savings account
- Play contract bridge (with another man and woman!)

Blue Movies

One hot stud trick with the chicks that I've found always works is to watch blue movies beforehand. Among the hottest in my collection are: *The Boys in Blue* (Cannon & Ball): very sexy indeed. *Danish Blue:* a public-information film by the Danish Cheese Board, telling the fascinating story of Danish cheese, from cow to creamery. *The Blue Lamp:* another very sexy film indeed. *Blue is the Colour:* the official story of Chelsea football club. *Blue 147:* a scintillating look at some of the great blue-ball shots played on the snooker circuit over the last ten years.

WELCOME TO MY HAREM

Here it is, my perfect love nest! What woman could resist a bordello as tempting as this!

Romantic Sights

A list of romantic sights invariably includes the old staples: Rome, Venice, Paris, the Taj Mahal, the Midnight Sun . . . Why not be original and go for some really interesting romantic vistas instead?

- Romford market on a Wednesday
- A snooker table on which the reds have broken perfectly to set up a possible maximum break (this is *my* favourite!)
- A perfectly re-tipped cue (no, hang about, *this* is my favourite!)
- JiFs Record Shop, 244 Chadwell Heath High Street
- Any Little Chef
- Qualifying round of the Rothman's Grand Prix at the Redwood Lodge, Bristol

CHAPTER 3

SNOOKER AROUND THE WORLD

One of the devil-may-care perks of being a top-flight international high-octane snooker player like me is the great opportunities you get to travel. By the time I was sixteen I had been to Stoke-on-Trent and Leicester, and just a year later I had made my first trip abroad, to Wales, and spent a week in Llanelli.

I fell in love with Wales at first sight – what a place, no wonder it's called Monte Carlo of the North – and ever since then I have often thought I might retire to a bungalow in Wales when I'm finished with the game. That's if I feel zany enough to cope with the twenty-four-hour-a-day hectic lifestyle everyone in Wales seems to lead. It's certainly no surprise to me that Terry Griffiths comes down to London every week for a rest!

Of course it wasn't long before I was going further afield than just Barry Island in my globe-trotting extravaganzas. In a whirlwind few months I visited Preston, Sheffield, Reading (twice), King's Lynn, Melton Mowbray (service area) and Felixstowe. I was really starting to spread my wings.

Nowadays my travels take me even further, and thanks to snooker I have been lucky enough to see parts of the world other people can only dream of. Wherever I go I keep my camera handy, and over the years I've had the chance to build up a pretty glamorous photo album of my travels. Here are a few of the shots from it. I hope you won't be too jealous when you see some of the amazing places I've been to!

STEVE'S REALLY INTERESTING PHOTO ALBUM

Me taking in the spicy nightlife in Bangkok.

Me sightseeing in Toronto.

Abu Dhabi. This was my first taste of Arab culture, and as you can see from the photo it was quite a shock.

Sydney, Australia. People say Sydney is one of the world's most attractive cities, and this shot certainly proves the point.

Rio was one city I'll never forget. Here we see the Copacabana Beach (from inside the main snooker hall).

In 1986 we were lucky enough to visit China. There was so much to see and photograph, but I think this shot captures the place perfectly.

Interesting Focus on Snooker 1

Chinese snooker
Chinese snooker has the same number of balls as normal snooker, it's just that they all look exactly the same.

Indian Rules Snooker
In Indian Rules snooker there is a newsagent on each corner instead of a pocket.

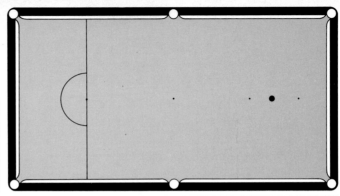

Interesting Focus on Snooker 2

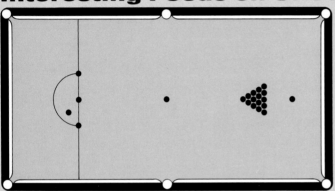

Snooker in Russia
In Russia a shortage of balls means each table has only one ball – a red (of course). There is no cue ball and no colours. Players take it in turn to simply pot the red. (Maximum recorded break: 1.)
(In Russian snooker the winner is always the one who is in the KGB.)

Air Travel
I really enjoy air travel. I don't know why, I guess I must just be one of those lucky, shoot-to-kill, go-ahead guys who can really appreciate the wild side of flying. Here are my tips for spicing up your flight to really make it interesting:

1. Start by taking your Ian Allen plane-spotter's handbook along with you on the plane and memorize all the facts and figures about your aircraft. Then get someone to test you on your memory. Recently I played this game with my manager Barry Hearn on a flight to Japan. I won when he threw the book down the toilet and tried to strangle himself as we passed over the Arctic Circle. For added fun you could try to memorize the statistics of a different plane from the one you're flying in. This is really interesting. Sometimes you can ask the air hostess to join in. Just stop her when she is serving the in-flight meal and ask her if she has got time to test you on your knowledge of the wing-tip measurements of the Convair 440. I bet you'll be surprised by how keen she is to help you.

2. When your in-flight meal arrives, stop the air hostess and ask her for the menu. Airline food is usually pretty exciting and it's good fun building up a collection of the menus from the flight meals you've eaten. I've got seventy-three so far, and am always on the lookout for new ones. In fact, I've even started a swap club to swap my doubles with other air travellers.

3. One of the most exciting things about flying is the in-flight movie. If you want to be really interesting and crazy why not do without the earphones and try to lip-read the story instead. This will save you at least £2.50 and is a lot of fun. Always try to make sure someone you know has actually got a set of earphones so you can ask him what was said if you miss a bit or get in a tangle. The other week it was Mel Brooks's *Silent Movie* and I kept nudging Barry to ask what was being said. We did laugh. Or at least I did.

4. Another thing I really enjoy doing on a long plane journey is watching the engine going round. Of course, this isn't quite as easy with a jet engine, but it can certainly be a lot of fun on propeller-driven planes. I sometimes challenge Barry to a game. He has to write down how many times a minute he thinks the propeller is going round, and I have to do the same, then we see who is right. Barry seems to have the knack of doing this while asleep. Unfortunately, we've never been able to find a way of working out who is correct, although on one flight we were travelling with Alex (Higgins) and we almost managed to persuade him to climb out on to the wing with a pen and paper to do a quick count, when the pilot rushed out and screamed at him to shut the emergency door and get inside.

5. My final interesting tip is pretty reckless, so I don't advise you to copy me unless you're really into skating on thin ice. What I do is when the air hostess comes down the aisle with the boiled sweets I take one from her and put it in my mouth. Then when she's gone I take it out again and wrap it in a piece of tissue paper. When she comes back again a few moments later I then tell her she missed me first time round and could I please have a sweet like everyone else. This way I get *two* sweets instead of one. Of course the first one usually has bits of tissue paper stuck to it and tastes like the inside of someone's trousers, but then when you live life in the fast lane you have to pay a price.

On the road

Nowadays I am driven in a chauffeur-driven limousine, but I haven't always been so dull. Years ago, when I really was a hotheaded million-miles-a-minute tearaway, I used to drive every boy-racer's dream: an Austin Maxi!

CRAZY BUT TRUE

My favourite motorway is the M25. This is a great motorway because it's round and has the same shape as a snooker ball, so you never come to the end. This means you could keep on driving round and round and round forever without stopping, if you wanted to (although obviously you'd run out of petrol after a few hours). (And obviously you'd have to spend twenty hours every day queuing to go through the Dartford Tunnel.)

Barry gave me the car as a present, and I don't think I've ever been as happy as when I took it for my first thirty-five-miles-an-hour burn up on the Romford ring road that very same day. Talk about crazy, here was the next James Dean!

Of course, some of the things I used to get up to in that car probably sound pretty hotheaded and unbelievable nowadays, but it's funny, at the time they just seemed normal.

For instance, sometimes I'd go round to my friend's house and because his father was out I'd park in the driveway. Of course if his dad came back I'd have to move the car to let him in, but that just didn't seem to matter in those wild-horse days, and even to the present day I can remember the crazy look my friend gave me when I first told him I'd done something really daring and parked my car in his dad's drive.

Another time I'd drive into town and spend two or three hours just

Barry's motor when I first met him. I guess it was this car that instilled me with my abiding love of thoroughbred motorcars

driving up and down the ramps of the local multi-storey car parks in Romford. Sometimes I'd go up and down the same ramp fifty or sixty times, but I didn't care, I was young and tempestuous and that was just my tearaway style.

Still other times I'd drive around the streets of Romford, slipstreaming the local dustcarts, then pulling out and zooming past them like a madman. I guess there are still a few refuse men around today who can remember the spin-the-dice, live-or-die loonie in the superfast Maxi!

Sometimes, if we were going to a function, I'd persuade Barry to leave his car at home so I could take him in mine and show him a few fancy tricks I'd been learning. I remember one night in particular, we had been to a snooker championship on the west side of London and were driving back along the North Circular Road when we reached the traffic lights at Gypsy Corner. Suddenly something inside me just flipped, and, after waiting for the lights to turn safely to green, I took off the handbrake, hit the gas and raced away like a lunatic till I was soon doing nearly forty-two miles an hour, then I slowed down again. Barry was so shocked he didn't say anything. No wonder he now calls me Crazy Horse.*

The Matchroom Cadillac

No it's not a joke, this is our Matchroom limo. Of course, a car like this can set you back thousands, but there's no reason why you can't enjoy the thrill of owning a limo just the same as this, thanks to the *Matchroom Do-It-Yourself Stretched Limo* kit (only £39.95).

KIT INCLUDES:

1. One fretsaw
2. Template for extra body parts (you should use plate steel, but reinforced cardboard can be used at pinch, provided you don't intend going out in wet weather)
3. One large tube of very strong adhesive
4. One sticky-backed Matchroom logo
5. One chauffeur's hat
6. One stick-on waving hand, for those who can't afford a chauffeur and have to drive themselves.

Tinted Windows

For that final authentic touch you should give your car tinted windows. Genuine tinted windows cost a fortune, but you can save most of that by using a roll of coloured cling film. Stick the coloured cling film to the inside of the windows to produce that tinted effect. It looks great, plus it can come in handy if you need something to wrap the leftover picnic food in when you're in a hurry, or if you find yourself caught without a protective (Tony Knowles).

*Actually, he doesn't call me Crazy Horse, but he could very well have started to after an incident as crazy as that!

THE
147S

THE GREAT SOUND OF BRITISH MOTORWAYS

M25(2"45') M2(1"10') M10(38') M42(Northbound
(1"23') M34(45')(Sliproad) M61(52') M508(6"12'
(Cats eyes) M6(Southbound)(2"38') M52(Con-
traflow)(1"27') Watford Gap Service Area
(3"52') M12(closed for re-surfacing) (3') M25
(reprise)(43') M9(concrete mix)

Motorways are Interesting

A great deal of my crazy life is spent travelling to and from events, so I get to see quite a bit of motorways. This is lucky, because motorways are just my kooky scene. That's why last year I was thrilled to discover a new double-album in my local record shop (Romford Wall of Sound) entitled *The Great Sound of British Motorways* and featuring the sounds of seventy-two different British motorways! You can bet it's got pride of place in my collection!

Not only is the record great to listen to, it can also be used for a pretty crazy-as-anything game. A group of friends sit around the room, you play a snatch from one track and, when the music stops, they have to guess which motorway it is. The winner is the person who guesses the most number of motorways. The game should last about three hours to make it really exciting. When you've played all the tracks on one side of the record you should start on the second side. If you're really feeling way out you could play the 'rugby' version. The same rules apply, but if you get the answer wrong you have to drink a pint of Horlicks. The winner is the last person left awake (usually lasts about twenty minutes).

And, talking of games, here is one I invented myself. I know I should keep it to myself and sell it for lots of money, but money doesn't mean anything to me and anyway I'm just so excited by it that I've decided to share it with you now. Here goes.

You start by writing down the name of every motorway in Britain on a little card. Then you shuffle the cards into a pack and each person takes it in turns to pull out a card. He or she then has to say where that motorway goes from and to. (You may need a road atlas to check.) This game can go on for hours.

(Hint: For a change you could play the game with B-roads. This is very difficult and is ideal for people who really know their roads. A foreign version can also be played if you have foreign guests in the house.)

Finally, although this book certainly isn't here to plug anything, I will make an exception, because it's not often I find something so good it literally takes my breath away. But that's what *Trivial Pursuits Special Motorway Edition* did. Over 10,000 questions, all about motorways. That's one madball fun-zone Christmas present I'd recommend to anyone.

JUST FANCY THAT!

Being a motorway buff, I bet you won't be surprised to learn that one of my favourite groups is Autobahn (that's German for motorway). I'm always amazed at how life is full of crazy coincidences like this, aren't you?

An Interesting Map of the World

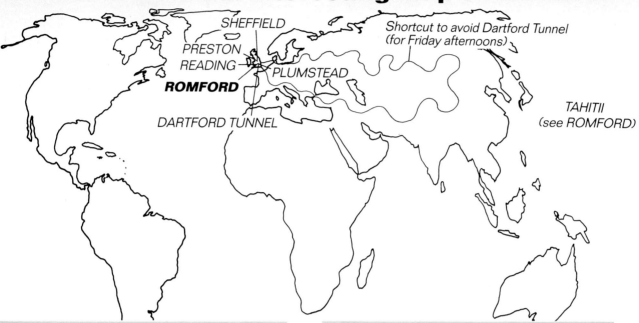

SHEFFIELD

PRESTON

READING

PLUMSTEAD

ROMFORD

DARTFORD TUNNEL

Shortcut to avoid Dartford Tunnel
(for Friday afternoons)

TAHITII
(see ROMFORD)

Interesting Things to do in Sheffield

1. Play snooker.
2. Visit the hotel coffee shop.
3. Visit the hotel bar.
4. Visit the hotel coffee shop again.
5. Visit the hotel shoe-cleaning machine.
6. Read everything in the complimentary guest pack in your hotel room.
7. Read the fire instructions in your hotel room.
8. Read the Gideon Bible in your hotel room.
9. Visit the hotel coffee shop again.
10. Travel up and down in the hotel lift pretending to be a spaceman.
11. Try to use up all the coffee and tea sachets in your hotel room.
12. Fiddle with the TV set in your room until you lose the picture altogether and have to get the manager in to fix it.
13. Travel up and down in the hotel lift, stopping at every floor and jumping out, then jumping in again before the doors close.
14. Steal the 'Do Not Disturb' sign from your hotel room.
15. Press all the lift buttons, then get out and use the stairs.
16. Put the shower-curtain on the outside of the bath and soak the floor.
17. Drop your keys down the lift shaft.

Interesting Things to do in Preston

1. Play snooker.
2. Visit the hotel coffee shop.
3. Visit the hotel bar.
4. Visit the hotel coffee shop again.
5. Visit the hotel shoe-cleaning machine.
6. Read everything in the complimentary guest pack in your hotel room.
7. Read the fire instructions in your hotel room.
8. Read the Gideon Bible in your hotel room.
9. Visit the hotel coffee shop again.
10. Travel up and down in the hotel lift pretending to be a spaceman.
11. Try to use up all the coffee and tea sachets in your hotel room.
12. Fiddle with the TV set in your room until you lose the picture altogether and have to get the manager in to fix it.
13. Travel up and down in the hotel lift, stopping at every floor and jumping out, then jumping in again before the doors close.
14. Steal the 'Do Not Disturb' sign from your hotel room.
15. Press all the lift buttons, then get out and use the stairs.
16. Put the shower-curtain on the outside of the bath and soak the floor.
17. Drop your keys down the lift shaft.

Interesting Things to do in Reading

1. Play snooker.

CHAPTER 4

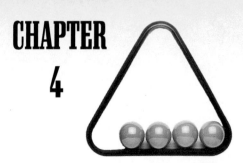

DOPE TESTING

Dope testing is now a part of the snooker scene. But too few players realize the amazingly interesting opportunities this presents them with. For instance, few players appreciate that you're legally entitled to ask for your sample back after any urine test and you can compel the official responsible to return any specimen to the organ from which it was removed once the test has been completed. WPBSA headquarters are obliged by law to keep all unclaimed urine for a period of three months. If at any time during that period you wish to reclaim your sample, you can contact them direct and ask for it to be forwarded on to you. You may also apply in person but it is always wise to note what yours looked like to speed up collection.

If you are asked to give a sample of your urine, then use the opportunity to your full advantage. Ask the official concerned to hold the sample bottle on the top of his head ten yards away, informing him casually that you've been doing it this way for years, and haven't missed yet. Promptly miss.

Alternatively, insist that a five-gallon container be obtained, pointing out that once you start you're not a tap and you just can't switch it off. Point out that you are not prepared to suffer the consequences of major flood damage. When the container is at last presented, take it to the toilet, fill it brimful with fresh tap water and secrete a couple of live goldfish (cunningly concealed till that point in your trouser pocket) into the container. Return the container to the official concerned with a passing comment that 'that little lot is better out than in'.

You may wish to request unusual or exotic assistance when giving your sample. Tell the official in charge you cannot pass anything unless there is a brass band present playing a selection of works by the great brass-band composer, Sousa. Point out that it is a childhood foible you have never grown out of and that you have an LP featuring the best of British brass at the ready in your own loo expressly for this purpose.

THE SHIP IN A BOTTLE TRICK

Retire to the toilet to provide the sample requested. Ignore persistent requests for you to emerge, claiming these things take time. Eventually reappear some eight hours later brandishing the sample bottle in which a model ship is now displayed. Should the official present become abusive or rude, complain indignantly that it isn't your fault if they fail to explain themselves properly.

Point out that as an old sea-dog your natural reaction upon being given a bottle to fill was to insert a ship inside, and that never in all your time afloat have you ever come across a 'urine in a bottle', bejabus me old hearties, yo ho ho and a bottle of rum.

Tips when carrying false sample bottles

1. Do not be over-ambitious. A jumbo-sized lemonade bottle filled with urine is likely to draw attention, including that of the TV cameras, and may lead to

detection or unpleasant gossip. Besides, there is little fun in spending six hours at the table with a five-litre bottle of urine in your pocket.

2. Do not use a hip flask to conceal your sample. There is a real danger you might mistake the flask for the real item and inadvertently take a sip from the sample, adding new meaning to the phrase, 'a drop of the wee stuff'.

An Interesting Story about Urine Tests

In a contest last year, Alex Higgins was asked to produce a sample for the contest doctor. However, try as he might, he just wasn't able to come up with the liquid goods. Luckily a sharp-eyed official was able to come to the rescue and, rushing off, returned a few minutes later with a large rubber plant, a posse of press photographers and several members of the WPBSA board.

'OK, Alex, try this,' shouted the official above the hubbub, and put the rubber plant at Alex's feet. Within seconds Alex was directing a rich fountain of flowing gold into the plant's roots in front of the gawping gallery. Zipping up his flies with pride, a few seconds later he handed the rubber plant across to the waiting doctor and marched confidently away.

Note: I tried to confirm this story with Alex but could not get an answer. When I eventually did get through it was to his answering machine, who complained that it had been out at Stringfellow's all night and it wasn't taking any messages and anyway who did I think I was calling at half past eleven in the morning.

Another Really Interesting Story about Urine Tests

Dennis Taylor's radical glasses were as much a product of the statutory urine testing as performance on the baize. Up until the time of the first tests Dennis had not bothered too much about his eyesight, but that all changed when one day he was marched into the doctor's room to give a sample and, reaching out, took a swig from one of the bottles.

He immediately spat out the contents and gasped bitterly that this was the last time he drank Australian lager. Gently it was explained that this wasn't the hospitality room and what Dennis had drunk was not Aussie lager but a touch of the other amber nectar, so to speak. After he had got over the shock Dennis took the whole episode in good spirits and admitted he should have known it wasn't Australian lager the moment the first drop passed his lips, because Australian lager didn't usually taste as good as that. (I'd like to point out that this is in no way meant to be derogatory to Foster's Lager for whom I do a lot of sponsorship and are absolutely brilliant and never brew a bad pint — Do you think this is enough of a plug, Sue? — Steve.)

Jimmy White and Urine Tests

Jimmy is as fast off the table as he is on it. His record at filling the bottle is 0.0035 seconds and has yet to be beaten.

Eddie Charlton

I was once with Eddie when we were both picked out to give a sample. I remember sitting in the doctor's room waiting for Eddie, who was to go first. Poor old Eddie, he took ten minutes sighting up his distances, measuring his aim and checking the line. Finally he was ready, and he stood up, unbuttoned his flies and missed the bottle by six feet.

An Interesting 'Spot the Ball' Competition

Can you spot the missing ball in the picture that follows?

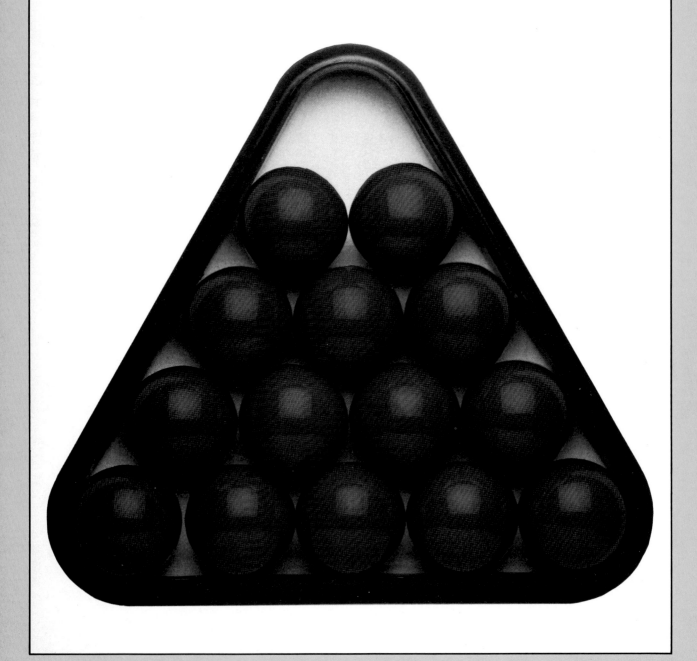

PENTHOUSE

SNOOKER TABLE PETS OF THE MONTH

My ideal Pin-Ups

● Mandy is twelve feet long, and has antique turned mahogany legs and brass pockets.

● Susi has played around with some of the top players. Now her ambition is to have Tony Knowles's balls in her pockets.

● Helga is hot and ready and finished in beautiful dark oak with English-leather pockets.

● Jo Jo's career really took off when she took part in the Benson & Hedges Masters at Wembley. Now she travels round the world on exotic assignments.

INTERESTING PEOPLE

CHAPTER 5

I'm lucky, I'm interesting, I'm outrageous. But I've not always been so interesting. Hard to believe, I grant, but there was a time before I joined the Plumstead Aeromodellers Club (Junior Section) when I was, dare I say it, a shade boring! No longer though.

You know, there's a misplaced belief that you are either born interesting or not. How wrong. The only way to be interesting is by working at it. Think *interesting*.

Every morning when I wake up to my toast and Marmite soldiers and grapefruit segments, I promise myself to do at least one interesting thing that day. Perhaps it will be an interesting chat with the heating engineer who's come to give the central-heating boiler its annual service, or maybe I will write an interesting letter to a science-fiction bookshop to ask for a catalogue.

One interesting incident a day soon adds up, and you'll be surprised when before long your life is one helter-skelter rollercoaster of wild events.

My second tip is to look around at other interesting people you admire to see how they do it. Here is my own hall of fame. Of course, everyone's choice is different and this is just my selection, but I bet if you asked around you'd find the names on this list cropping up time and again.

THE TEN MOST INTERESTING PEOPLE IN THE WORLD

Name the ten most interesting people in the world? A difficult task? No, not for a crazy, hip-shooting high-baller like me. Selecting the ten most interesting men is simple. All ten stand head and shoulders above the competition. Taking each of the devil-may-care loonies in turn, I come up with:

Nick Owen

Nick's my idea of an interesting guy. I remember we once shared a taxi to the railway station after a recording at TV-am (my idea of an interesting TV station!), and on the way Nick told me all about his private collection of rare football programmes, and his secret desire to play in goal for Coventry City. After that he just had to go top of my list of livewire hellraisers. And yours!

Arthur from *EastEnders*

I don't get too much time to watch TV, travelling round the country like I do, but when I get the chance to put my globe-spinning feet up, then there's one show I like to watch more than any other: *EastEnders*! Divorce, suicide, drink, drugs. It's amazing how they've summed up life in London so convincingly. And there's one person who really makes that show tick: Arthur. He certainly knows how to stir the pot of life and liven things up a bit. I especially like it when we go down to Arthur's allotment and see him potting something, and watch him cracking up!

Derek, the Manager at the Matchroom Club

My number one, five-mile-high, solid gold champion. He's the only topsy-turvy, rough-and-tumble, live-for-today jetsetter who keeps a written record of every teabag in his tea caddy. Now, that's living!

David Vine's brother-in-law

I always thought David Vine was a pretty crazy guy, until I met his brother-in-law! He works for British Telecom (Peckham District), and an evening spent listening to his hellraising stories of the zany, mad capers a telephone engineer gets up to quite takes the breath away.

The Man who Reads the Local News Headlines on Anglia Television

Some people may be surprised by this choice, but I've been a big fan for years, and never miss him. In fact, even when I'm away from home I always make a point of videotaping the local news headlines so that when I get back off tour they're there for me to watch.

The Man at the Exhaust Centre who Fixed Barry's Car

I suppose when you're in the exciting world of car-exhaust repair you naturally turn out interesting. The man who fixed my manager Barry Hearn's car spent over two hours telling me about his new bathroom suite and how he'd gone for the low flush pedestal-type toilet basin, even though the man in the shop had recommended a different one. And you can't get more interesting than that. Or can you?

The Chairman of Peterborough United Football Club

Again, some of you may think this is an oddball choice, but you don't get to be Chairman of a blue-chip top-drawer team like Peterborough unless you've got that extra-special something going for you.

The Man who Sells Hoover Accessories in Plumstead Saturday Market

Anyone who can make Hoover parts sound interesting is certainly a hot contender for a place on my list. I used to walk past his stall every day on my way to snooker practice, and I'd often stop off for a wild and crazy hour's chat about replacement vacuum cleaner parts. You don't forget an outrageous experience like that easily!

© Woodland Animations Ltd 1985

Postman Pat

OK, he may be a puppet, but as puppets go he's totally outrageous and really knows how to live on the wild side and fill his life with crazy fun. Postman Pat Postman Pat and his black and white cat… crazy lyrics, crazy man!

Bob Wilson

Bob is my idea of a natural ball of fun. I've been a fan of his for years, so you can imagine how thrilled I was when I got to meet him at a sportswriters' dinner recently. 'Hallo Steve,' he said straight away, in his silky smooth voice. Then he spent two hours telling me all about cutting down the angle for the approaching forward. What a crazy, live-for-kicks guy.

David Vine

Call me a supercharged hothead if you like, and most people do, but for my money there can't be a more interesting person than David Vine. Perhaps I'm biased, but we just seem to have a natural rapport. 'Tell us about that tricky blue in the fourth frame.' 'How did you feel when you went down 9–7 in the second session?' 'Tell us what you were thinking when you saw that final red go in to leave Alex needing snookers.' I don't know what it is, but David and I just seem to share the same brand of electrically charged live-wire conversation whenever we meet.

And the fantastic thing is it's been like this ever since we first met. I can still remember David's first incredible words to me as a raw eighteen-year-old: 'Tell us what was going through your mind when Terry left you on for that difficult pink along the top cushion.' I suppose I knew even then we would get on.

THE DAVID VINE FAN CLUB

Last year I was proud and privileged when David asked me to be president of his fan club. Of course I accepted the honour at once, and since then the club has gone from strength to strength, attracting at least three new members, two of them still alive. The club provides a focal point for members to keep in touch and there is a thriving video section where members can swap videos of David's latest interviews.

I think David's greatest strength is that he is such a totally versatile presenter. One minute he's introducing snooker highlights from a chair in one studio, then the next minute he's introducing skiing highlights from a chair in a completely different studio. He really is *that* adaptable. Add to this if you can his almost uncanny ability to ask the right question at the right time, swinging the conversation around from asking how someone felt when they missed an easy black, to asking his opponent how he felt when he missed an easy blue. That's what I call an all-round presenter.

Finally, add in to this highball cocktail David's way-out-west wardrobe of outrageous sports jackets, each one even more outrageous than the last, and you can see why he is such a star.

And yet, despite his fame, David has somehow remained deeply unassuming in his popularity. Sitting in the car park in his X-reg. lime-green Talbot Horizon, eating his complimentary BBC lunchpack (jumbo sausage roll, packet of cheese Wotsits, Vimto and a Wagon Wheel) he rarely attracts even a passing glance. And for such a high-profile personality, believe me that takes real skill!

Now You Too Can be Like David

Just follow the instructions below and you too can share the thrill of *being* David Vine. You will need:

A rubber plant
A chair
A coffee table
A pair of glasses
A television camera
An autocue machine
A David Icke blow-up doll to pass all the mundane daytime links to

Arrange the chair and the coffee table in front of the television camera, with the rubber plant alongside. Put on the glasses and sit in the chair, saying nothing. At half past three in the morning look in the camera and say, 'Well, that's the end of our snooker coverage for this evening, but we'll be back with further coverage of this enthralling contest in a little over eight hours from now.' Continue to do this for a full two weeks, then stop. As an alternative, you can say, 'Well, we've got a few moments before the players come out for the next session so while we wait we thought we'd show you a little piece of fun the boys here in the backroom have put together.' Try to chuckle while you're speaking. Keep chuckling for several hours afterwards.

Dave 'n' Ron

Lots of people, including me, are fascinated by this dynamic duo that have captured the hearts of the nation in their *Superstars* competition. What is their secret? Ron puts it down to their brilliantly contrasting styles: 'David isn't fat, and I am.'

Others point to the fact that Ron wears the short-sleeved shirts that are a bit too tight around the arms, which bulge out, whereas David wears the glasses.

Whatever the secret, these two are here to stay!

Incidentally, Ron's bio reveals he is almost as versatile as David; he used to be a thin middle-distance runner, but now he's a fat commentator! That's what I call changing horses in the middle of the stream.

For those who are interested there is a David and Ron fan mag available, plus a range of exciting gifts for the Dave 'n' Ron fan, including a Dave 'n' Ron mug, a 'Dave 'n' Ron sunstrip (can be Ron 'n' Dave for continentals), a Dave 'n' Ron Do It On The BBC At 6.45' car boot sticker, a 'Dave 'n' Ron Do It on Spikes to the Nearest Tenth of a Second' car bumper sticker and a 'Dave's the Fave and Ron's the One' window sticker (sizes: small (4"x5"), medium (10"x12") and billboard (15"x47")).

DAVE 'N' RON

Dare to be David Vine

There are few universal truths in this topsy-turvy rough-and-tumble world we live in. But there is one I know is true: you won't find a more interesting character than David Vine. And I don't suppose there'll be many people arguing with that statement! After all, what could be more interesting than introducing *Ski Sunday* every Sunday, plus a new series of *Superstars* with Ron 'Call-Me-Mr-Zany' Pickering? Not a lot, I hear you reply.

Now I can offer exclusively to you a unique chance to actually *be* David Vine. That's right, you can be Dave the Rave in the comfort of your own living room, thanks to this remarkable David-Vine-ophone.

Below is a real interview between me and David. We have deleted all David's lines so you can take over. All you do is ask the questions you think David might have asked me and there you are, right in David's open-toe sandals and herring-bone underpants!

Hmm, now that's what I call living in the hothouse!

CAST: Me = me
DAVID (YOU) = you

DAVID (YOU):
Me: It's a pleasure.
DAVID (YOU):
Me: That's right.
DAVID (YOU):
Me: Yes.
DAVID (YOU):
Me: Well, one option was to pot the yellow and screw back up the table in the direction of the blue to try the green with the rest into the bottom left-hand pocket, but instead I decided to go for the strong run-through off the yellow which would take the white off the side and bottom cushions leaving myself closer to the green, David.

DAVID (YOU):
Me: No.
DAVID (YOU):
Me: That's right.
DAVID (YOU):
Me: I think probably leaving Alex a free ball in the fourth frame of the afternoon session when I'd just started to get the upper hand in the safety exchanges, and then missing that vital pink to leave myself needing snookers later in the frame.

DAVID (YOU):
Me: Yes, having to come from 6–3 down in the quarters against Jimmy.
DAVID (YOU):
Me: Remove the split ring washer through aperture B and loosen the main metal grommet before carefully inserting a new ¾" rubber washer to the inside of the main sprocket casing with the self-tapping screws provided.

DAVID (YOU):
Me: No, only if the sheep's owner objects.
DAVID (YOU):
Me: Thank you, it's a pleasure

TEN INTERESTING THINGS YOU DIDN'T KNOW ABOUT DAVID VINE

1: Me 2: David Vine 3. An early prototype of David Vine (never developed)

1. David Vine's real name is, in fact, 'David Vine'.

2. David Vine has a bank account under the name David Vine.

3. David Vine first shot to international acclaim as host of the world-famous TV show, *Quizball*.

4. David Vine's catch phrase is, 'And now over to our experts in the commentary box.'

5. David Vine is a founder-member of the David Vine fan club.

6. David Vine once forgot his bag in a hotel and had to go back and collect it the next day. (If he was really interesting he'd have had it sent on, as I did when it happened to me!)

7. David Vine is a leading world authority on the bus ticket.

8. David Vine wears odour insoles in all six pairs of his Clarke's Trekkers.

9. David Vine has never done a free-fall parachute jump off the Eiffel Tower (this information correct at time of going to press, 8.8.1988).

10. David Vine's parents originally thought about calling him Neville, but changed their minds at the last minute because they thought it was too daring.

A HANDY HINT
Here's a handy hint for budding DVs everywhere. First, bone up on a still-to-be-discovered sport: cribbage, progressive whist, off-ground-tig, ludo, etc. Now pop along to Milletts and kit yourself out with a mustard-brown sports jacket, a trendy brown-and-brown striped kipper tie, and a set of three-inch-angle-iron-rimmed spectacles. Now approach a TV station with a view to presenting a weekly programme about this sport. And hey presto, that's it, next stop top glam-boy sports presenter!

TRICK SHOT

An important part of the modern game is exhibitions, and one of the most popular parts of these is the trick shot. I have now built up quite a crazy repertoire, and dotted through the book you'll find examples of quite a few. Here is my first:

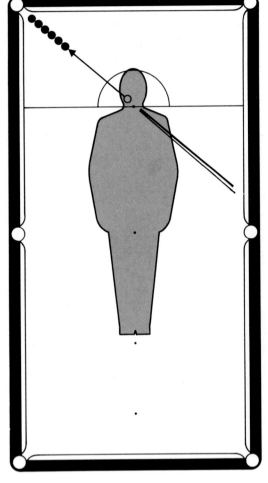

In this shot I ask a member of the audience to come forward and lie with his back on the table and his head in the 'D'. I now place the ball in his or her mouth and the target ball is placed at the end of a line of reds across the jaws of the bottom pocket.

I then strike the cue ball, giving it plenty of top. This should take it clear of the mouth. Meanwhile, I allow the cue to travel through to enter the person's nose, which clears the sinus passages and neatly trims any nasal hair. It then de-waxes both ears, removes any belly-button fluff, dislodges any hard or callused skin from the ball of the foot and does a quick inspection of the teeth, arranging an appointment for a check-up with the dentist if necessary. In addition, the cue tip lathers and shaves the person's chin before finishing off with a full manicure. At the same time the cue ball cannons into the line of reds and pots the black into the pocket.

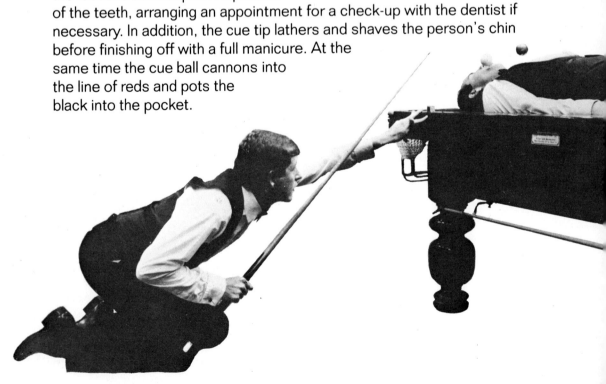

CHAPTER 6

INTERESTING THINGS TO DO WHILE YOU WAIT FOR YOUR SHOT AT THE SNOOKER TABLE

The thing that marks the card of the really interesting person (e.g. me) is his ability to find interesting things to do in otherwise not-quite-so-interesting situations. And nowhere is this more apparent than when you have to sit waiting for your opponent to play. This is where I score high marks over my fellow pros. They invariably miss out by not seizing the opportunity to do something cheeky or unusual. Unlike me, always up to some hairy scrape.

Here are just a few of the interesting things I get up to and, as you can clearly see, it's quite a feast of fun. Now you can see why everyone in snooker agrees there's no chance of a dull moment when I'm around!

Wiping your Cue Clean

One of the questions that young players always seem to be asking me is who taught me to clean my cue with the cue cloth while waiting for my opponent to play his shot. The answer is going to shock you; no one helped me, I'm entirely self taught. In these days of mounting professionalism, that must sound a pretty outrageous statement, but believe me it's true. At no point have I ever received any coaching in the use of the cue cloth. I'm one hundred per cent self taught, and that will set tongues wagging, I'm sure.

Some players are not so lucky though, and need to keep working to polish their cue-cleaning technique throughout their life.

Just recently I was privileged enough to be approached by a major film company (the Romford Motion Picture Company, previously the Romford Mobile Kebab Shop) who wanted to make a special training video for young snooker players to show how to clean your cue with a rag correctly while sitting in your corner. Naturally, I agreed at once. Well, opportunities as good as this don't come up very often. And two weeks later the video, 'Use Your Rag' (my title, geddit?) by Steve Davis, was in the shops, price 27p.

THE MATCHROOM

Cleaning your Cloth / Correct use of Cue Cloth

Snooker fans will be interested to know that I have just recently made a video showing some of my best cue-cloth tricks. The video lasts fourteen and a half hours, and I reckon it's the definitive work on the subject. There I am shooting my mouth off again — what a wild guy!

Just as players stay with the same cue throughout their careers, so most top pros build up a great attachment to their cue cloths.

I normally hold the cue firmly and rub it up and down with Eric.

This is my cue cloth. It's called Eric, and has been with me for eight years.

Recently, some players have adopted the highly controversial technique of moving the cue through the cloth, with disastrous results.

Eric sleeps underneath my pillow, where the magic pixies protect him and keep him safe.

Don't use a portable washing machine to clean your cue.

SNOOKERTIP SERIES

And don't get carried away and put on a pinny and start cleaning the table, the chair and the rest of the auditorium.

Me experimenting with a new cloth, 1978.

The Age of the Micro. Me with the latest State-of-the-Art Sinclair Micro Cue Cloth (the CC5) in 1982.

Interesting Ways to Chalk Your Tip

(This gets my vote for the most interesting title in the book – Steve)

Call me rash, call me mad, call me outspoken, call me an out-and-out sensationalist, but to my mind there is nothing more satisfying in life than a well-chalked tip, and nothing more interesting in the game of snooker than the act of chalking up before every shot. I suppose it is the high-risk thrills and danger that appeal to me the most. The knowledge that one is literally looking into the jaws of death every time one puts the chalk to one's tip gives this its irresistible appeal. Even a top-risk sport like Grand Prix motor racing can't compete with chalking one's tip when the chips are down and the big stakes on the table!

You want proof? Well just look at some of the frightening things that can happen.

1. The chalk could spontaneously combust and send a giant fireball racing across the table. All right, it hasn't happened yet, but there's a first time for everything. Believe me, this is one accident just looking for somewhere to happen, and when it does I will be the first to say I told you so.

(Incidentally, for practice sessions I now use the patent fire-proof chalk container. It may be a shade on the large size, but I want to see it tomorrow!)

2. A razor-fine splinter of chalk dust as sharp as any dagger could shear off from the main block and fly out and pierce a player's chest. This is a very real threat. Don't be deceived by the fact that chalk is normally very crumbly. Under certain extreme atmospheric changes (like a giant meteorite storm, or Armageddon) there is a chance the chalk could undergo an extreme molecular change, in which it hardens to the strength of tungsten steel and becomes a lethal weapon. Obviously the scenario for this accident might seem to depend on an unlikely sequence of events, but the world has to end at some time, and why not during the first round of the World Team Championships at Bournemouth? I for one believe this is a very real threat.

3. The block of chalk could become inadvertently wired up to the National Grid by some simple everyday error and you could pick up a fatal electric charge the moment you touch it. Unlikely, you might think, but it's just the sort of accident that happens all the time and we never see coming. All it takes is for an overworked electrician to enter the snooker hall where you're playing and mistakenly remove the chalk block from your pocket and wire it up to the main ring main. Or perhaps the electricity board are laying high-voltage overhead cables in the area and mistake your chalk for an electricity pylon. At the moment there is absolutely no protection to stop an accident like this occurring. At no stage are spectators searched for electrical tool kits and there is absolutely nothing at all to prevent a rookie sparks from making such an elementary gaffe. All we need is for one leading snooker player to be killed by an electrified chalk block and there will be a public outcry, but at the moment the authorities and everyone in the game seem blind to the dangers. (Except me.)

4. A meteorite could crash through the roof of the snooker hall and kill everyone present. Admittedly, this isn't directly connected to chalking one's cue, but there's no reason why it shouldn't happen just as you are chalking your tip, which therefore becomes ancillary to the cause.

An Interesting Anecdote about Alex

One of the things I'm most known for on the circuit is my quick wit and lively tongue. No wonder people are always saying, 'When will that Steve Davis shut up?' I guess it's just the way I am; a compulsive chatterbox. I've always got some nutty story or anecdote to tell! And through this book I'll share them with you. Starting with this one, about Alex.

One of the funniest stories about Alex happened a few years ago, when I found myself with a few hours to spare before my next match in the Benson & Hedges Masters at Wembley. Strangely, Alex was free too, and he announced he was going to go out and buy a new shirt and would I like to go with him as he always liked to make sure he was buying the right thing.

I had nothing else to do, so I agreed and we set off in Alex's car to Jermyn Street, where Alex had been told he could have a shirt made. We eventually parked the car on top of an ornamental fountain and entered the first shop we came to.

'Hallo,' said Alex, as the tailor walked over. 'I'd like you to make me a shirt with different coloured cuffs and collars,' and he handed the tailor a wallpaper catalogue to use as a pattern.

Of course we were both a bit upset when we opened the paper next morning and discovered that the shirtmaker had committed suicide by throwing himself under a bus. And at the time we both felt a little guilty when we heard that the tailor had left a note saying he wouldn't have been able to live with himself if he'd made a shirt for Alex, but looking back, the whole story certainly makes me laugh.

LEARN WITH STEVE
Correct Sipping of Water

YOU SHOULD NEVER LEAVE ANY ASPECT OF YOUR GAME TO CHANCE, AND NOWHERE IS IT MORE TRUE THAN PICKING UP YOUR GLASS

YOU WILL FIND AS YOU PICK THE GLASS UP THAT YOUR FINGERS TIGHTEN UP AND THE HOLD BECOMES A GRASP. IF YOU GRASP TOO TIGHTLY TOO SOON YOU WILL NOT BE ABLE TO TIGHTEN LATER AND WILL LOSE A LOT OF NATURAL FEELING THAT HELPS YOU GLIDE THE GLASS EFFORTLESSLY TO YOUR MOUTH

I ALWAYS HOLD THE GLASS WITH MY THUMB AND FIRST TWO FINGERS. THE OTHER 2 FINGERS ARE JUST RESTING AGAINST THE GLASS AT THIS STAGE, THERE SHOULD BE NO TENSION IN THE HAND, THE GLASS HELD LOOSELY BUT SECURELY. HOW YOU HOLD THE GLASS WILL DEPEND ON ITS SIZE; NORMALLY MY GRIP IS 3/8MM FROM THE RIM

IN THE FINAL STAGE THE LINE OF THE KNUCKLES SHOULD BE ROUGHLY HORIZONTAL. MINE IS IT NOT CONSIDERED TEXTBOOK SIPPING AS I OFTEN ALLOW MY MOUTH TO MOVE TOWARD THE GLASS AT THE LAST MOMENT. REMEMBER NO WATER SHOULD EVER PASS THROUGH YOUR LIPS WHEN SIPPING LIKE THIS

I NORMALLY RECOMMEND THE GLASS LEAVES THE MOUTH AS SOON AS A CONTACT HAS BEEN MADE WITH THE LIPS. THIS RELEASES THE HAND TO CLEAN MY CUE AND RUB THE SIDE OF THE NOSE. THE DESCEND PATH OF THE GLASS SHOULD BE RELAXED AND SMOOTH AND RETURN THE GLASS TO EXACTLY THE SAME SPOT IT WAS BEFORE SIPPING. THIS ALLOWS YOU TO REPEAT THE ACTION

CHAPTER 7

OTHER INTERESTING SPORTS

I know this is going to sound pretty rash and bold, but then, I've never been one to hold back from controversial remarks, have I? I believe there are other sports that are interesting apart from snooker! There, I've said it, shoot me down in flames as a headline-seeking, publicity-courting, wild sensationalist if you must, but this is my sincere belief and I stand by it.

The trick is to identify the key roles that make the sport really interesting. Here is my list of these sports and the gilt-edged positions to go for.

SPORT	POSITION
Darts	The scorekeeper
Ten-pin bowling	The scorekeeper
Yacht racing	The man who fires the starting pistols
Football	The substitute goalkeeper
Tennis	A ball-boy
Cricket	The square-leg umpire (not Pakistan, where very uninteresting indeed)
Golf	A caddie
Croquet	A player
Ice hockey	The goalkeeper
Boxing	The man who holds the bucket
Crown Green Bowls	The physiotherapist
Curling	Absolutely anyone at all
Clay-pigeon shooting	The pigeon. Or the man who pulls the target

Interesting Sports to Follow

The other trick is to look beyond the present sports field to new and interesting sports. Among those which have caught my fancy are: deck quoits, Cumberland wrestling, beagling, real tennis, shoveha'penny, synchronized chess.

Potholing

I was recently invited to take part in a new TV series of pro-celebrity potholing. It was only when I arrived fully equipped with cue and dress suit at the venue (a deserted windswept outcrop on the North Yorkshire moors) that I realized the pot referred to was a hole in the ground and not a pocket on a table, and this was one 'pot' I couldn't 'hole' with a snooker cue (geddit?).

Nevertheless, making the best of a bad job, I quickly strapped on the boots and helmet provided and set off underground. (Incidentally, in case you're wondering, yes, I did take my cue with me, just in case we found a snooker table down there – and, no, we didn't.)

I must say the 'hole' thing (geddit) was incredibly interesting and I was won over in minutes. Put simply, the idea of the game is to climb down a deep hole, get wet, then climb back out again.

Of course, there's a lot more to it as well. For a start you can get stuck (interesting), cold (also interesting), or lost (extremely interesting).

My favourite part of all was sitting frozen to the core in an underground chamber with flood water rising up to our necks while we waited for the rescue team to come and get us out. This was extremely interesting.

Incidentally, when I'm at a tournament and can't get away, I sometimes practise my pot-holing by climbing around inside Bill Werbenuik's stomach. I often spend three or four hours inside his tummy.

Billiards, are You Man Enough?

Billiards is a pretty crazy, high-powered game, so always check with your doctor that you're fit enough before taking it up. Remember that billiards is very similar to snooker, except there are only three balls and no one ever watches it. Here is my potted (geddit? Aren't I 'pun crazy' in this chapter?) guide to the three-ball game. In billiards points are scored by: 1. Striking the white cue ball onto your opponent's white and red ball (a cannon). 2. Striking the white cue ball into the pocket off another ball (an in-off). 3. Potting your opponent's red or white ball (a pot).

4. Agreeing to pack it in and play a game of snooker instead (a good idea).

Example of a Very Interesting Sequence of Scoring Shots in Billiards

in off/cannon/pot/cannon/in off/pot/pot/ cannon/in off/cannon/pot/cannon/cannon/ pot/in off/cannon/in off/cannon/pot/in off/cannon

Example of an Even More Interesting Sequence of Scoring Shots

cannon/cannon/cannon/cannon/cannon/cannon/cannon/cannon/ cannon/cannon/cannon/cannon/cannon/cannon/cannon/cannon/cannon/ cannon/cannon/cannon/cannon/cannon/cannon/cannon/cannon/cannon/ cannon/cannon/cannon/cannon/cannon/cannon/cannon/cannon/cannon/ cannon/cannon

A hint: Billiard breaks can last far longer than those in snooker. I suggest you always keep a five-year diary handy so when you're not at the table you can mark the days off.

How to Make Billiards Even More Interesting

Add another fourteen red balls, a yellow ball, a green ball, a brown ball, a blue ball, a pink ball, a black ball, remove one of the white balls and call it snooker.

Travel Billiards

Travel billiards allows you to enjoy all the thrills and spills of billiards while out on the road. Simply take a conventional house brick and keep hitting yourself over the head with it. You'll be surprised just how similar to a game of billiards it is.

Crazy but True!

Crazy but true, I could have missed out on a snooker career because of table tennis. That's right, there was a time when I preferred the take-a-tumble high-risk sport of ping pong to the sport of snooker. I suppose it's easy to see why: the glamour, the excitement, the charisma, the sparkling jet-set bright-lights world of the international ping pong circuit can easily attract a susceptible twelve-year-old like I was. I remember the bribes that were made to entice me to join Plumstead Junior B, then a go-ahead outfit in the Crayford and District Sunday table tennis league. Free bus fares, a new bat and a Kit Kat after every match. With big offers like that on the table it wouldn't have been at all surprising if I'd swallowed the bait and taken up the offer, turning my back on snooker. And what a change of fortune that might have meant!

I suppose it must have been fate that intervened and took a determined hand, because the very next week the Plumstead Junior B manager ran off with a woman from the all-night chemist and that was the end of the team. I was back at the snooker hall next day, the ping pong bug crushed forever.

Of course I still play table tennis whenever I can and pride myself that I still turn in a match for most people. The ping of the ball on the table, the squeak of a freshly cleaned pair of rubber soles on the linoleum floor. Who could resist that? And with my hellraiser, good-time, hells-a-poppin' image, ping pong is just the sport to suit!

Unfortunately, my travels mean I'm not always able to get to a table-tennis table when I'm on the road, so I've devised the brand new sport of *Pocket Ping Pong*. It's just like ordinary ping pong, with all the thrills and spills of the full-size game but now you can play it anywhere.

Here's how it works.

Pocket Ping Pong

On the facing page you'll find twenty-four 'cards', twelve pings and twelve pongs. Cut them out and shuffle them into a pack, then deal the cards into two packs of twenty-four cards. Place the packs face down in front of the two players, who then take it in turn to take a card from the top of their pack. A ping must always follow a pong, and vice versa. A point is lost when a player draws the wrong card. Of course, you can broaden the game to doubles by dividing the pack into four and taking it in turns to 'play' your shot.

Play must always start with a 'ping'. Players offering a pong must try again. Two 'pongs' mean a double fault, and the service reverts to your opponent. The cards are shuffled and re-dealt after every point. Normal table-tennis scoring applies.

I have played this game a hundred times, and it never ceases to be fun. You could even be really outrageous and arrange whole pocket ping pong championships between your friends and family, as I do. In fact, every time I try to play Barry he ends up throwing his cards in the bin and telling me I've won, that's how good I've become.

With this game in my pocket there's no danger of me ever being dubbed a dullard.

Note: Foreign versions of the game can be made for 'international' matches. For French version insert le before each word: le ping, le pong. For Italian version insert il: il ping, il pong. For 'adult' version insert ****ing before each word: ****ing ping, ****ing pong.

THE EVERLASTING VERSION
For an 'everlasting' version, simply make all cards the same: all pings. This game is really interesting because you can keep playing it all day without the rally ending.

PING	PING	PONG	PONG
PING	PING	PONG	PONG
PING	PING	PONG	PONG
PING	PING	PONG	PONG
PING	PING	PONG	PONG
PING	PING	PONG	PONG

Fishing

When I want to relax, one of my favourite hobbies is fishing. Not that there's anything relaxing about the sort of angling I do! As one of the country's top gudgeon fishers, when I cast my line anything could happen. And usually does!

Having caught your fish you may be wondering what to do next. Here are my tips for the ten most interesting things to do with a fish.

1. Throw it back into the water and catch it again.
2. Measure it with a ruler and send the details to *Angling Mail* for inclusion in their 'Fish Of The Month' section.
3. Kill it.
4. Eat it.
5. Tickle it (trout only). (Important: Never try to tickle a piranha.)
6. Stuff it. (Never try to stuff a live fish. You are likely to end up with a fish that has a very broad grin that makes it completely unsuitable for display except to a BBC sit-com audience. Never try to stuff a tin of salmon.)
7. Train it to ride a unicycle. (Very difficult, but more impressive than 6 or 5.) (Or 4, 3, 2 or 1, for that matter.)
8. Put it in your Keep Net and keep it there until you're ready to go home. (Not suitable for thirty-feet killer sharks with razor-sharp teeth.)
9. Smoke it. (Fish are usually smoked in a smoke oven or over a smoke fire. Don't attempt to put a live fish in your mouth and light it with a cigarette lighter.)
10. Dress it. (Suitable for crabs — crustaceous kind only — lobsters and prawns. A dressed fish is one dressed for eating. It doesn't mean you have to take a pilchard and put it in a jumper and trousers.)

CATCHING GUDGEON – with STEVE DAVIS

I FIRST FIX THE MAGGOT TO THE END OF THE LINE. SOMETIMES I LIVEN THIS BIT UP BY HOLDING MAGGOT RACES BETWEEN TWO MAGGOTS ROUND THE TOP OF MY BAIT BOX LID.

MAGGOTS

NEXT I CAST MY LINE AND WAIT FOR A BITE.

THIS CAN LAST SEVERAL HOURS AND IS VERY INTERESTING. THEN SUDDENLY THE FISH TAKES A BITE AND THINGS REALLY START TO HAPPEN

LANDING A FISH LIKE A GUDGEON CAN BE VERY DIFFICULT AND I FIND A LARGE LANDING NET IS VITAL TO HELP BRING THE FISH IN

NEXT STEP IS TO REMOVE THE HOOK FROM THE FISHES MOUTH. THIS IS THE PINNACLE OF THE DAY'S FUN.

THEN I THROW THE FISH BACK INTO THE WATER AND START ALL OVER AGAIN.

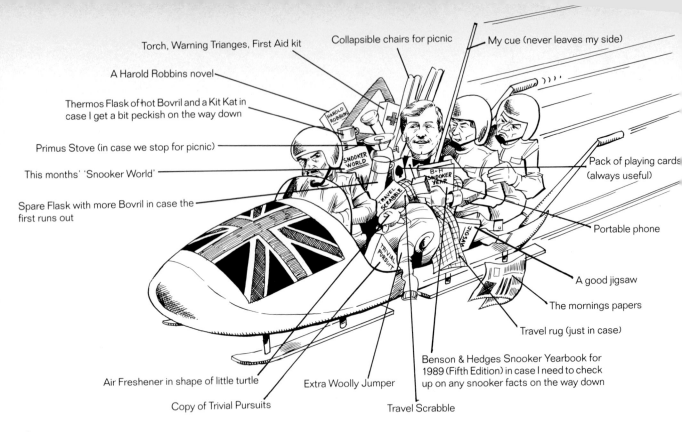

Torch, Warning Trianges, First Aid kit

Collapsible chairs for picnic

My cue (never leaves my side)

A Harold Robbins novel

Thermos Flask of hot Bovril and a Kit Kat in case I get a bit peckish on the way down

Primus Stove (in case we stop for picnic)

This months' 'Snooker World'

Spare Flask with more Bovril in case the first runs out

Pack of playing cards (always useful)

Portable phone

A good jigsaw

The mornings papers

Travel rug (just in case)

Air Freshener in shape of little turtle

Extra Woolly Jumper

Benson & Hedges Snooker Yearbook for 1989 (Fifth Edition) in case I need to check up on any snooker facts on the way down

Copy of Trivial Pursuits

Travel Scrabble

The Bobsleigh

Last year I was lucky enough to be offered a free ride in the British four-man bobsleigh for a ride down the Cresta Run. Although it was a lot of fun, I must admit that I was slightly disappointed, as I'd thought it was going to be more interesting than it turned out.

At first I couldn't work out why it failed to excite me as much as I'd anticipated, and then the truth hit me: while the front man (driver) and the rear man (anchor) have quite a bit to do to keep them occupied, the other two members of the team were left with very little to do.

That was when I had a sudden rush of blood to my head and the wild idea of livening up the bobsleigh hit me.

Here is my 'new look' bobsleigh, complete with additions and amendments. Some of you may think I've been too reckless and gone a bit wild, but no one could ever complain that a ride in this 'bob' is dull!

Another Interesting Anecdote About Alex

Another interesting 'Alexdote' concerns an occasion when we were both playing in the 1982 Langs Scottish Supreme Masters. Alex had been having a little bit of domestic trouble and decided to cheer himself up and take his mind off things by having a couple of hours off. Once again, I was free and agreed to join him.

We decided to visit a nearby town in Alex's car and, after we had removed the rosebush from underneath the front wheel arch and made sure the other driver could get his car down from the tree, we popped into a television rental shop for a browse. I was looking at remote-control models when the assistant approached Alex and asked if he could be of service. Alex said he could and explained that he was particularly interested in renting a rubber TV set he could drop from the third storey of buildings without it breaking.

The assistant began to giggle nervously at this point, and made an excuse and disappeared into the rear of the shop.

You can appreciate how surprised we both were twenty minutes later when a new assistant came out in a terrible fluster and said the first assistant would not be able to serve us as he'd suddenly been taken rather peculiar and had decided to visit China and become a missionary. Alex then asked the new assistant if he could possibly help, but when he mentioned TV rental the assistant started to sweat profusely, picked up a nearby phone and began to check with a local travel agent on the price of one-way air tickets to the Pitcairn Islands.

Me going to a fancy dress party on my panto horse costume ably supported by Barry and Alex. Guess which is which

Here I am receiving a trophy after my dog 'Interesting Boy' won the top race at Romford. Barry later went on to manage the dog and made several important changes including covering it in green baize, stretching it to twelve feet long, and putting pockets on each corner

A Final Interesting Alexdote

This final Alexdote concerns the time they wanted to do a TV show with Alex, called *A Round with Alex*. The idea was that each week Alex would drink a different celebrity under the table. A pilot was planned and Oliver Reed invited to take part as the celebrity.

Unfortunately, after six days' serious drinking neither party was anywhere near under the table, and it was decided to abandon the whole series while the drinks bill was still under £10,000.

Boxing
My Tips for Making Boxing More Interesting

Since Barry started to promote boxing matches, I've taken quite an interest in the sport. Indeed, it's not widely known, but for the Bruno v. Bugner fight that Barry put on I was in fact Frank's regular sparring partner and put him down on the canvas several times in training.

The thing that strikes me most about boxing is how much difference a clean broom would make. Look at the amount of snooker on TV (3 million hours in 1987) and compare it with the amount of boxing (22¼ hours). Snooker put its house in order and has never looked back. I reckon boxing can learn a few lessons from this.

My Tips for Improving Boxing
1. **David Vine.** Boxing doesn't have a colourful character like David Vine to set it alight and catapult it on to the world stage. I firmly believe that if boxers were obliged to sit next to a rubber plant after every fight chatting to David then the audience figures would leap ahead.

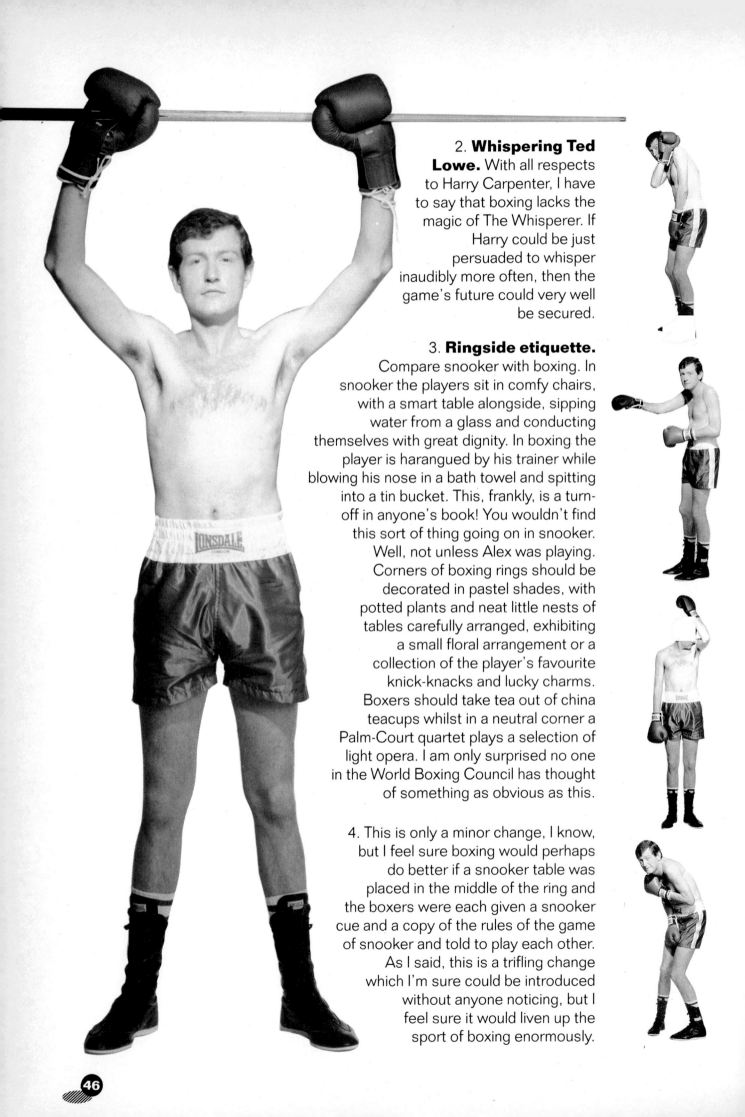

2. **Whispering Ted Lowe.** With all respects to Harry Carpenter, I have to say that boxing lacks the magic of The Whisperer. If Harry could be just persuaded to whisper inaudibly more often, then the game's future could very well be secured.

3. **Ringside etiquette.** Compare snooker with boxing. In snooker the players sit in comfy chairs, with a smart table alongside, sipping water from a glass and conducting themselves with great dignity. In boxing the player is harangued by his trainer while blowing his nose in a bath towel and spitting into a tin bucket. This, frankly, is a turn-off in anyone's book! You wouldn't find this sort of thing going on in snooker. Well, not unless Alex was playing. Corners of boxing rings should be decorated in pastel shades, with potted plants and neat little nests of tables carefully arranged, exhibiting a small floral arrangement or a collection of the player's favourite knick-knacks and lucky charms. Boxers should take tea out of china teacups whilst in a neutral corner a Palm-Court quartet plays a selection of light opera. I am only surprised no one in the World Boxing Council has thought of something as obvious as this.

4. This is only a minor change, I know, but I feel sure boxing would perhaps do better if a snooker table was placed in the middle of the ring and the boxers were each given a snooker cue and a copy of the rules of the game of snooker and told to play each other. As I said, this is a trifling change which I'm sure could be introduced without anyone noticing, but I feel sure it would liven up the sport of boxing enormously.

CHAPTER 8

ME AND BARRY

I could write a whole book about Barry. But for now I've got to make do with a chapter. So I won't waste any more time. I'll just say that this is a selection of the most interesting stories about me and Barry.

Barry and Snooker

Despite his close involvement in every aspect of the game, Barry isn't a great snooker buff when it comes to peformance on the baize.

I can vividly recall the first time I met him at the Lucania club. I used the club regularly for practice and Barry had heard I was a bit handy around the table, so I was taken into his office to meet him. Formalities over, I agreed to go back into the hall and give Barry a quick demo of my skills.

As we opened the door to the clubroom Barry froze dead.

'What's that?' he said, pointing at a snooker table.

'It's a snooker table, Barry,' I replied.

Next moment he was giving it the optical once over, wanting to know why there weren't any chairs to go with it for the diners to sit on. Then finally he threw a real wobbly and started pulling at the cloth, saying it was a terrible colour for a tablecloth and he should know because he used to be in the rag trade and anyway why was it nailed down like that, and the only good thing about it was the edging to stop the knives and forks falling off.

In the end everything was explained and Barry calmed down, but I still don't think he's quite come to terms with the game.

Occasionally, for fun, I'll ask Barry to play a frame against me. This is always awkward. Barry usually starts by asking what he's got to do. I explain he's got to hit the white ball with his cue, so he leans across the table and taps the top of the ball with his cue, sniffing with contemptuous ease and calling out, 'OK, your turn, Davis.'

I pointed out that the idea is to hit one of the red balls with the white ball, at which point Barry's face lights up and he picks up the white ball with his hand, taps it on top of the red ball and calls out confidently, 'OK, Steve, how many points do I get for that?' before complaining that the referee was slowing the game down by putting all the balls back on the table.

Finally I explain that the idea is to knock the white ball into the red ball with your cue, at the same time knocking the red ball into the pocket. This is where Barry goes off for a notebook and pen to write it all down.

Barry usually leaves me to myself at a big championship. 'The tactics are your area, Davis,' he always tells me. But if things are really getting hot or tense he will sometimes step in with a word or two to help.

Generally the advice is to pocket as many balls as possible.

'If you can just get the balls in the pockets in the next session then I think we could win this one,' he'll tell me knowledgeably.

One of the things I admired most in Barry were his collars. Not only were they extremely fashionable, but if he had to bale out of an aircraft without a parachute at 25,000 feet then he was able to glide down to earth unharmed

Barry well on the way to his maximum break of -7

Barry tries to play a tricky shot with his cue box from underneath the table

'I fancy balls in the pockets in the next frame, Steve,' he'll confide with a knowing nod of the head.

I remember going out for my epic final with Dennis Taylor a few years ago with Barry's advice still ringing in my ears: 'If you can just score more points than him in every frame then we've nothing to worry about.'

Despite his problems in coming to terms with the game, Barry is still one of its biggest fans. Many's the day I'll get up in the morning and Barry will rush into my hotel room, clearly in an excited state.

'Did you see that game of snooker on the telly last night?' he'll scream, jumping up and down and tugging at his chin. 'Bloody brilliant, this geezer there, wiped the floor with everyone, brilliant, tall bloke, thin, red hair . . .' Then I'll have to point out that it was me, and what he'd been watching was a video I lent him of my 1984 triumph in the final of the Lada Classic.

'Bloody marvellous stuff,' he'll continue breathlessly, missing the point entirely. 'You ought to give him a game sometime!'

Then he'll rush out again to tell the rest of the Matchroom boys.

I suppose if Barry's got one ambition in life it's to better his maximum break to date of −7.

Barry's Early Years

Barry's now a highly successful promoter, but I bet most of you didn't know that he actually started out in the rag trade.

Barry claims he was an accountant and that he was only involved in the bookkeeping side of the business, but I have my doubts and have a sneak theory that he may also have modelled men's cardigans. I didn't have any direct proof of this until a couple of years ago when I entered his office to find him parading up and down in a new jumper and posing extravagantly in front of a camera and tripod arranged in the corner of the room. Naturally I tackled him about it, but he assured me it was nothing and that he always tried on new cardigans in this way. Of course I believed him totally at the time, but a few days later when I found him doing the same thing in a chunky lambswool sweater and matching pom-pom hat, complete with pipe, well, I must say, my suspicions were aroused.

He wouldn't actually spill any beans, and instead concocted a story that it was a secret hush-hush project he was working on in connection with a new WPBSA deal he was fixing up, and that not a word of it should

Barry still squeezes in the odd bit of catalogue work when he has the time. Here he models a formal evening outfit for an Albanian mail-order catalogue.

Barry often works evenings as a singing telegram. The money's good, plus he gets free use of the outfit in his spare time. Here we see him surprising a convent of nuns with his version of *The Desert Song*.

leak out to anyone. He then broke down in tears and started to mutter that it wasn't fair that Roger Moore had got the breaks while he hadn't and that Roger had never looked nearly as good in cashmere as he had. And then he brought out a portfolio of modelling shots and spent three hours telling me why he should have been cast as James Bond and that anyway Roger had looked terrible in that balaclava on the modelling assignment to Switzerland in '59 and that he, Barry, had saved the day by modelling it himself.

Of course I swore an oath of secrecy and have never once let a word of this out to anyone, but I'm sure as loyal readers my confidence is safe with you.

Barry celebrates after winning third prize in a rabbit-modelling contest. Barry still keeps his ties with the modelling world.

Barry and Promoting

Barry is one of the most successful promoters in the business. No, correction, he is *the* most successful promoter, full stop.

But promoting is a very stressful business and the effect can be dramatic. There was one incident that is etched in my memory as vivid proof of this. Barry had been up all night discussing a very important shampoo deal for Willie Thorne, to be named 'Shoulders' and was clearly not feeling himself when I visited him in the Matchroom next day.

I think it illustrates very clearly the pitfalls any budding promoter has to face and stands as a cautionary tale.

I have put together this account of the actual incident from my memory and from the office transcript. It was about 10.30 in the morning and I entered Barry's office with the coffee tray and the official Matchroom biscuit barrel, to find BH studying the top of his desk intently.

Barry: So, clinched deal to promote my ashtray, stepped in as promoter of my biro and agreed to act as joint co-promoter of my paperclip holder – hmm, not a bad morning's work there, Barry –

Me: I've made you a cup of coffee, Barry.

Barry: And now you'd like me to promote it?

Me: Eh?

Barry: You've made a cup of coffee but you haven't got a promoter for it, so you're turning to me for help?

Me: It's just a cup of coffee, Barry.

Barry: Exactly, it's just a cup of coffee now, but if the right promoter gets hold of it, all that could change overnight.

(At this point the phone rings. I pick it up. It's Barry's wife Susan.)

Me: Barry, it's your wife.

Barry: Ask her if she wants me to act as her promoter.

Me: No, Barry, she just wants to speak to you.

Barry: And does she want me to promote the fact that she wants to speak to me?

Me: Barry, she just wants to know what you'd like for your tea.

Barry: (Getting agitated) Who's promoting this tea?

Me: Nobody, Barry.

Barry: Which is why she's keen that I step in as promoter!?

Me: Barry, she doesn't want you to act as promoter, she just wants to know what you'd like for your tea.

Barry: Hmmm, so she's got some other promoter in mind, has she?

Me: No, Barry.

Barry: No promoter in mind? Her manager ought to get that sorted out.

Me: Barry, she doesn't have a manager.

Barry: I see, so what she'd really like is for me to step in as her manager and arrange her day-to-day affairs, at the same time fixing up a promotional deal along the lines she has just suggested?

Me: No, Barry.

Barry: How can she say no, I haven't even told her the terms.

Me: She doesn't want to know the terms.

Barry: Aha. Shrewd thinking. I like it. Leave the deals to me. She does the business in the kitchen, I do the business on the business side.

Me: Barry, she says can't you forget the business talk for just a minute?

Barry: Wait a minute, does she want me to write that into the contract?

Me: There isn't a contract, Barry.

Barry: You mean, it's not binding?

Me: What?

Barry: You're confident that we can talk to the lawyers and find a way out of the contract?

Me: What contract?

Barry: Exactly! What contract! By the time our brief has been through it, it will be torn to pieces.

Me: Barry, she says can't you forget the promoting nonsense just for five minutes and tell her whether veal cutlets will be all right.

Barry: All right, look, tell her I've got a few phone calls to make; world TV rights, video sales, the cutlets' fee, residual rights for the potatoes, the price structure for the gravy, the corporate image of the peas, exclusivity of the napkin ... availability of Wembley stadium ... Tell her I'll call her back in five

(At this point Barry's missus rings off.)

Me: Have your coffee and bikkies, Barry.

(I hand over the biscuits to Barry, who surveys them earnestly.)

Barry: Right, so when do they want me to start acting as their promoter?

Barry after he'd taken part in a mammoth four-day currython for charity. Barry managed forty-six vindaloos and raised nearly £21.60 in the process.

Barry's Business Brain and Boxing

Boxing is now big business, and Barry's business sense has been much in demand in this arena. Luckily, he is quick to think on his feet and has been able to bring his business brain to the task.

One-Man Boxing

Half the purse, double the profit. And because there's no knockout, the man in the ring can go on all night and save having to book a support. Plus no ref. fees or seconds. An absolute winner!

Boxing for TV

Barry believes we should radically re-think boxing along TV lines. Thus, one twenty-minute round, then a three-minute break for commercials. Plus staggered starts to allow maximum live worldwide TV coverage. One boxer starts at 9.00 p.m. British time, the other five hours later, at 9.00 p.m. American time. Plus a more TV-orientated line up, including pro-celebrity boxing, where the boxers fight a famous celebrity (Marvin Hagler v. Curly from *Coronation Street*, Mike Tyson v. Bonnie Langford, Earl 'Bonecrusher' Graham v. Stevie Wonder).

Barry also believes there are great opportunities for introducing boxing into other TV programmes. Among his suggestions are:

1. *Songs of Praise*; parishioners should be able to request a boxing match in the middle of the sermon instead of a hymn.

2. State Opening of Parliament to include a boxing match between the leaders of the House.

3. All future Royal Weddings to include six three-minute rounds on the balcony of Buckingham Palace immediately after the nuptials.

Barry on the way to becoming a successful cross country runner. Note the sleeveless vest which is the mark of a true pro, and a long way from the long sleeve cardie and crimplene trousers he wore when he started

Barry and Marathons

A few years ago Barry decided to get in trim. As a natural extension of this he took up marathon running. He is justifiably proud of his achievements and has many trophies and mementoes. This is one of his most valued trophies. It was taken to commemorate Barry's first appearance in the London Marathon and was especially commissioned by Barry to honour the event. It now hangs in the pride of place on Barry's office wall as a cherished testimonial of his finest hour.

CHAPTER 9

SO WHAT'S GOOD ABOUT ROMFORD?

What is the secret of this latter-day Babylon? This modern Jerusalem? This Valhalla of the Western World? For centuries philosophers and thinkers have toiled with the great mysteries of our world, but one question has constantly passed them by: why Romford? In this special supplement we explore the fascination of this eternal citadel, this jewel in Essex's crown, this elixir of all mankind, and explain its strange hypnotic powers of wonderment on all who go there.

RDWATCH ROMFORDWATCH ROMFORDWATCH ROMFORDWATCH ROMFORDWATCH ROMFORD...TCH

Getting to Romford

By air   Nearest airport, Romford International (aka Heathrow)

By rail   Pullman bullet train direct from Liverpool Street station (overnight couchettes available)

By bus   66, 86, 247, N99, Green Line 500

Romford bus depot. A bus leaves here for Hornchurch every seven minutes!

Famous Books about Romford

Jackie Collins, *Romford Wives*

F. Scott Fitzgerald, *This Side of Romford*

George Orwell, *Down And Out In Paris and London and Romford*

Nevil Shute, *A Town Like Romford*

Edward Gibbon, *The Decline and Fall of the Romford Empire*

The Romford Phrase Book

Useful phrases to use when visiting Romford.

* Where is the Romford shopping centre of which I have heard so much?
* No, really, I find the smell most appealing.
* What time is the next bus to Gidea Park?
* I am most impressed with the cashpoint machine outside Lloyds Bank.
* I have parked on the second floor of the multi-storey car park overlooking Debenhams.
* I am sorry I am late, but I have spent the last four hours trying to work out the one-way system.
* D'you fancy a burger and fries from The Starburger in the High Street?

Currency

The Romford pound. The unit of currency in Romford is the *Romford Pound (£R)*. Romford currency is absolutely identical to ordinary currency and has an exchange rate of one £R to the pound sterling. There is no restriction in the amount of currency that you can take in or out of Romford.

A Romford one-pound coin.   An ordinary pound coin.

ROMFORD CURRENCY-CONVERSION TABLE

£R	£sterling
1	1
2	2
3	3
4	4
5	5
6	6
7	7
8	8
9	9
10	10

(Correct at time of going to press)

The Romford Gifte Shoppe

Perfect gifts to take home with you as a reminder of your time in Romford.

1. A bottle of Eau de Romford toilet water, capturing the essential essence of all that is Romford
2. A Romford national costume doll
3. An individual gift-wrapped saveloy and chips from the Romford grill
4. A framed copy of the British Rail Romford to Liverpool Street train timetable
5. A genuine black plastic refuse-collection sack, as issued to all residents of Romford
6. A wall poster depicting the great road traffic signs of Romford

Of Special Interest

The NCP car park. Romford boasts one of the best NCP car parks in Romford, and from the top floor you command views right across Romford. A second feature that makes the Romford car park especially interesting is the unusual ticket arrangement. A white ticket is exchanged for a blue ticket, which is surrendered at the barrier. There is no other known example of this unique arrangement.

The Unofficial Town Motto
When in Romford, do as the Alsatians.

Romford from the Air
The great sights of Romford.

PLUMSTEAD
MY SORT OF TOWN

The Plumstead Fact File
● Plumstead was founded by the Plums in 1593.
● The twin town of Plumstead is Woolwich (because they couldn't find anyone else who would twin with them).
● Six people have been given the freedom of Plumstead. (Unfortunately, five of them didn't want it and handed it back, and the sixth one committed suicide on being told.)
● Plumstead is often described as the 'Gateway to Thamesmead'.
● Important dates in Plumstead:
  Labour Day (every Thursday down the job centre)
  Half-day closing (Mon. to Fri. inclusive)
  Glorious People of Plumstead Day (cancelled due to lack of interest)

Famous Films Featuring Plumstead
From Here To Plumstead
The Road To Plumstead (starring Bing Crosby, Bob Hope and the woman from the sports outfitters in the High Street)
Lawrence Of Plumstead (Lawrence of Arabia's adventures in Plumstead)
They Came From Plumstead (sci-fi thriller about a group of aliens who come from the planet Plumstead)
American Werewolf In Plumstead
Black Emmanuel In Plumstead (erotic soft-porn movie set around a bicycle repair shop in Plumstead)
Last Tango In Plumstead
From Plumstead With Love (the only James Bond movie to be set entirely on location in Plumstead)
The Plumstead Connection (a packet of Rennies goes missing from the mini-market in Carlisle Road and the police call in Popeye Doyle)
Flying Down To Plumstead (glamorous 1930s musical about a group of showgirls flying down to Plumstead for the season)
Passage To Plumstead
Casablanca (Plumstead) (remake of the classic Bogart movie, now set in Plumstead)
Plumstead, Plumstead (sequel to *New York, New York*)
Crocodile Plumstead

PLUMSTEAD JOKE
Q: Why did the Plumstead chicken cross the road?
A: Because that was his idea of a really good night out.

The Plumstead Walk
(lyrics)

Any evening any day
You will find us Plumstead way,
You'll find us all
Doing the Plumstead walk.

Into Smiths and out again
Waiting for a number ten,
Come and join the scene
In London South-East
Eighteen.

CHAPTER 10

HOLIDAY CHAT

With somewhere as altogether fab as Romford on my doorstep, you might well ask how I could ever drag myself away on holiday. Thing is, you'd be right, too, because every day I'm in Romford is a holiday.

But those of you not as lucky as I am might like a few tips on interesting holiday spots. So here they are, my holidays of a lifetime.

The Norfolk Broads. East Anglia on the water. Fun, sun and several interesting road junctions.

Anglesey. Are you man enough?

Wales. Home of the Wellington, the leek and Max Boyce.

The Isle of Man. Anywhere with a capital city called Douglas is worth a visit.

Weston-super-Mare. My only complaint is they got the name wrong; it should be called Weston-Brilliant-Mare.

Budleigh Salterton. The most exciting place I know after Shepton Mallet.

Belgium. Home of the Flems. Especially worth a visit: Ostend during the snooker championships.

The Isle of Wight. Watch the tide come in or don't watch the tide come in, the choice is yours.

Bulgaria. Here's one country that certainly knows how to rock and roll.

An early photo of me promoting holiday brochures. In this deal I agreed to work for half the fee if I was allowed to keep the jacket.

Me on Holiday
in Shepton Mallet.
I was eventually
thrown out of
the pub after a
4-hour break,
at bar billiards

My favourite holiday snap

Me on holiday on
the Isle of Man

Interesting Things to Do and Say at the Hotel

● Go up to the reception desk and tell the girl that the television isn't working in the bridal suite.
● Ask the head-waiter at the Savoy Grill if they take luncheon vouchers.
● Go up to the doorman at the Ritz and ask him if he can park your bicycle for you.
● Complain to the manager that the shoe-cleaning machine has just eaten up your Hush Puppies.
● Complain to the manager that the hostess tray in your room hasn't got any Bovril.
● Ask the reception desk if they have any snooker videos on the hotel's movie channel.
● Walk over to the reception desk and say, 'I'm sorry, I've just dropped another room key down the hotel lift shaft.'
● Phone up room service and order a boiled egg and ten soldiers.
● When the woman asks what paper you'd like, ask if it's possible to have the *Romford Recorder*.

CHAPTER 11

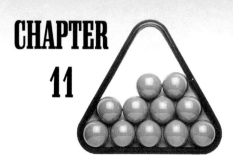

MY GUIDE TO THE STARS

JIMMY WHITE
Full name: Jimmy Fitzroy Lucan-White
Birth sign: Silk Cut
Favourite food: Twenty Rothmans
Favourite drink: Packet of Rothman's Top
Hobbies: Greek philosophy
Favourite TV programme: *Highway*
Favourite holiday: Rambling holiday in the Lake District
Most embarrassing moment: Being mistaken for Steve Davis

Jimmy White

I don't mind admitting that when Jimmy came on the scene, I was pretty jealous of him. After all, he had a nickname at the time and I didn't. In fact, after one tournament (or tournie as we hip cats like to call them) I went up to Jimmy and tried to pretend I didn't know he was called Whirlwind. He said, 'Hi, Steve,' and I said, 'Oh really, no, I didn't know you were called Whirlwind, Whirlwind,' as casually as you like. Of course that immediately let him know I was no mug.

Since those days, though, Jimmy and I have become firm friends and sometimes Jimmy even lets me go round to his house to try out his nickname. Of course, it feels odd being called Steve 'Whirlwind' Davis, but then I suppose Jimmy would feel a bit odd if he started calling himself Jimmy 'Interesting' White.

Jimmy's main problem off the table is timekeeping. I personally think he should change his nickname to Jimmy 'Not-Very-Good-at-Getting-There-on-Time' White, but Jimmy says he thinks that's a bit too long for a nickname. In fact, I think he may have thought I was trying to get him to change nicknames simply so I could steal his old one for myself, because ever since then he's made a point of saying things like, 'Hi, Steve, I'm still called Whirlwind,' and, 'By the way, Steve, did you know my nickname was still Whirlwind?' or even, 'Do you like my Jimmy "Whirlwind" White T-shirt, with the word Whirlwind on it, Steve Definitely-Not-Called-Whirlwind?' whenever we meet.

DENNIS TAYLOR
Full name: Sandra Jane Dennis Taylor
Birth sign: Fattie
Favourite food: Yes
Favourite drink: Yes
Hobbies: Yes
Favourite TV programme: *My Little Pony*
Favourite holiday: I'm sorry, I don't answer trick questions
Most embarrassing moment: Being charged excess baggage when I tried to take my glasses-case abroad

Dennis Taylor

Dennis was unable to come up with a nickname despite many years trying, the best he ever achieved being Dennis 'Tornado' Taylor. Unfortunately, anyone who has seen Dennis's frame in action will know that a tornado he is not, and after a brief period with the name Dennis 'The-Slightly-Plump-One' Taylor, followed by an even briefer period with Dennis 'If-I-Breathe-In-It-Doesn't-Look-So-Bad' Taylor, he eventually decided to drop nicknames altogether.

Fortunately, a few years later and still nicknameless, he hit upon the brilliant idea of ridiculous glasses as a 'nickname substitute'. It was an inspired move. Now everyone knows him immediately as the guy with the bicycle on his nose.

Three shots that prove the versatility of Dennis Taylor. 1. Dennis with glasses.

2. Dennis without glasses.

3. Dennis with glasses and bottle of champagne.

Since then, Dennis has never looked back; he's never looked forward or sideways, either, the only direction being a sort of strange eighty-degree squint at the ceiling.

In fact very few people actually know, but Dennis has got perfect 20/20 vision and the glasses are merely there for effect. In training without them he regularly scores ten or twelve 'maximum breaks' on the trot, and can go several days without missing a pot. Yet in championships, with the glasses on, he sacrifices shots galore. Such is the price a top snooker player must pay for his image.

Alex Higgins

Alex was the first player to have a nickname, and when I was just starting I remember being in great awe of him because of this. I knew if I got on the wrong side of him he could say things like, 'Oh it's Steve "No-Nickname" Davis,' or, 'Look over there, that's Steve "Without-the-Nickname" Davis,' or sometimes he would ask me how my nickname was, then start sniggering behind his hand. I suppose in many ways this was the start of the rivalry between us. Alex always had the upper hand because he had the nickname and no one else did, and then when other players started to get names, Alex got insanely jealous and his game went right off.

I suppose Alex's biggest fault lies in not changing his nickname to stay ahead of the group. I, for one, am surprised he never looked into the possibilities of sponsorship, and I could certainly see that the opportunities are endless; Alex 'Morphy-Richards-Pop-Up-Toaster' Higgins has always seemed an excellent name to me, and while I can understand him being unhappy about Alex 'Cleans-Round-The-Rim-Of-Your-Toilet-Faster-Than-Other-Bleaches' Higgins, I feel sure there must be other names that would suit.

Me with Alex Higgins shortly before his shirtmaker shot himself.

Cliff Thorburn

Cliff is an example of a nickname who came into the game late. For many years Cliff had been playing on the circuit without feeling the need for a nickname. Then all of a sudden there he was being called 'The Grinder' (a reference that surprisingly doesn't relate to Cliff's style of play, but rather to his extensive collection of the cheese graters that are his great passion after the game).

When a player suddenly receives a nickname like this it can have a disastrous effect. The nickname immediately goes to the player's head, and he loses his natural composure. Luckily Cliff was strong enough to withstand the pressures and emerged unscathed.

Cliff's other great advantage is his moustache, which has

become a sort of trademark. In fact the moustache is actually registered as a trademark for copyright purposes and if you look closely you can see the little registration stamp just to the left of his left nostril.

Again, it's not widely known outside snooker circles that the moustache is a fake and comes off after matches. It is curious to think that instead of being called 'The Grinder' (a good name) Cliff could well have ended up being called 'The Man With the Funny False Moustache' (a far harder name to live down). He didn't though, and in this, I'm sure, lies the secret of his success.

During championships a popular audience pastime is communal puffing in an attempt to dislodge Cliff's moustache from its perch.

Terry Griffiths

Terry has never been interested in nicknames, being quite content to devote all his energies to his hairstyle. Indeed, so important is the hairstyle that it now has its own management contract and has in the past demanded equal appearance money with Terry. However, I don't want to pre-judge anyone, and a look at the background is illuminating.

Terry comes from a small Welsh village and was eighteen before he first came across a hairstyle. Indeed, even to this day there are still people in Wales who have yet to see a decent haircut. You only have to look at Ray Reardon and Doug Mountjoy to realize this. All this despite the worldwide efforts of many charities set up to fight the appalling problem of Welsh hair fashions. The shock of seeing that first hairstyle left a deep mark on Terry, and for several years afterwards he attended weekly hairstyle counselling sessions to help him live as normal a life as possible for one so severely traumatized.

This early experience goes some way to explaining the problems Terry encountered with his hair a few years ago. He had become increasingly addicted to styling mousse and had in effect become a hair-conditioner junkie. He would give himself a 'fix' by putting more and more mousse on to his hair and he was becoming increasingly desperate and dependent on gel. He would regularly disappear into the bathroom with a shaving mirror and reappear two hours later with his hair moussed to a peak.

One morning Barry and I went into his hotel room to collect him for the day's play in the Mercantile and we found him collapsed under a huge weight of Wella shampoo. It was a terrible sight. There was foam everywhere and it was clear from the hundreds of empty bottles of Alberta Balsam littering the floor that he had been washing his hair for several hours.

We immediately rushed him to a nearby hairdressing salon and he spent the next four days drying out under a hairdrier. We contacted a top hairdresser and he confirmed our worst fears: Terry would have to stop using mousse on his hair or his roots would dry up in less than six months, leaving him completely bald. It was a terrible moment when we had to confront Terry with the raw facts and explain that it was either kick the habit or start having implants like Eddie Charlton.

Since then, of course, Terry has fought to stay off mousse and is on a medically controlled dose of Head 'n' Shoulders. The effect has been to stop his hair from becoming over-bouffant and while it now appears that Terry has got the whole thing under control and regained his form there is always the danger of a relapse, and undoubtedly this fear has affected Terry's position in the world ratings.

Terry Griffiths before he discovered his first hairstyle seen here holding his second prize cup for the 'Burry Port Head Of The Year' competition (1974). First prize was won by a hamster

Ray Reardon

Ray's biggest problem is that he is a Ray Conniff fan. I remember the first time I found this out; I was shocked. I was just nineteen at the time and had been playing in a competition in the north of England. Barry was with me, and as we stood at the bar he narrowed his eyes and told me now I was old enough to know, there was something that he thought I should be told. Then he whispered in my ear that Ray was a big fan of Ray Conniff and had several of his hit records.

It was a terrific shock. I had always known Ray had a 'naughty secret', but I had always believed this to be that he was a Mantovani fan, so when it was revealed to be much more serious and involved Ray Conniff, well, it completely shattered all my illusions.

For several weeks after the revelation I was inconsolable. I tried talking to people about it, but they just didn't seem to understand. In the end I had to accept that everyone was different and that liking Ray Conniff was just Ray's own personal hang-up. I simply had to tell myself that there was nothing he could do to help himself and that some men just needed to behave like this. It was sad, but there it was, and I wasn't going to do anything to change it.

The story would perhaps not merit a mention in this book were it not for the fact that still to this day I have a recurring nightmare where I find myself stranded at a snooker tournie and Ray offers me a lift home in his car. I gratefully accept, only to find that once in the car he pops a Ray Conniff's Greatest Hits tape into the cassette player and I am forced to spend the four-hour journey home listening to Ray humming along to it.

One of the questions everyone asks about Ray is how accurate are the Dracula rumours. The truth is that there is virtually no truth at all in the stories, and Ray very, very rarely bites anyone. In fact I personally have only been bitten by him three times, and the last time I wouldn't even have noticed if he hadn't leapt on to my back and started to claw at my neck.

Of course Ray knows all the vampire stories ('How would you like your stake?' 'Through The Heart.' 'just nipping out to the local Blood Donors for bite to eat...'), but luckily he is pretty level-headed and has a laid-back attitude to the whole thing, simply sinking his fangs into the neck of anyone who says anything offensive, and sucking out every last drop of blood.

Tony Meo

Tony and I were the first players Barry signed, so we go back together quite a long way. If we do have a problem it is that Tony doesn't like the German group Kraftwerk quite as much as I do. I remember that when their single *Autobahn* first came out, I was so impressed I bought a copy and played it eighty consecutive times on the tiny portable dancette record-player that I'd taken into our dressing room at the Hofmeister World Doubles in Northampton. In the end Tony just flipped and, leaping up from where he lay with a pillow over his head, he ripped the record from the turntable and smashed it to bits on the floor. At first I thought he was just joking, but then I saw he was foaming at the mouth and had gone as white as a sheet and I realized he wasn't fooling around.

I waited for him to stop his frantic war-dance on the shattered pieces, then reached into my bag. 'It's OK, Tony,' I said. 'That was your copy. I bought two, one for you and one for me; here's mine,' and I took out a second copy of the record from my rucksack and put it on the turntable. After that, Tony seemed to go a bit odd. He stormed out of the room and refused to speak to me again for three years.

Strangely, that is the only time Tony and I have ever argued, because usually we're the best of mates. In fact, when Tony got married I was the best man at his wedding and I was lucky enough to be able to pick up two more copies of the Kraftwerk disc at a backlist record shop as my present to the bridesmaids. Tony must have been very touched, because he tried to make me take them back, but I refused, saying it was just my little extravagance and it was only right they received something special to remind them of the day.

TONY MEO
Full name: Tony Theo Leo Theopolis Meo
Hobbies: Supporting Parathosolosolopolis United and being mistaken for a Greek
Birth sign: Kebab
Favourite food: Moussaka and vinegar crisps
Favourite drink: Taramasalata milkshake
Favourite TV programme: Nick Owen's *Sporting Triangles*

Tony Knowles

When I first started playing snooker my bottom came in for a lot of attention. I must say, this unnerved me at the time. I hadn't prepared myself at all for the interest, and apart from a small reference in John Spencer's book to 'wiggling your cutie' and 'take care of your butt' there was nothing in all the coaching manuals about botty presentation. So you can imagine my relief when Tony came along and took over the mantle as king of the bottom proclaiming himself the new arsehole of snooker.

In many ways Tony has made the botty audience his own over the last few years. His bot-bot now has a loyal and faithful following and is much in demand for exhibition matches, where a common game is for seven club players put their best cheek forward against Tony's in a winner takes all contest.

Indeed, so faithful have Tony's followers become that he has even been able to build up a thriving and well-run fan club on the basis of it. Members receive a fanzine with news of Tony's bum's latest achievement, together with details of forthcoming appearances by the bum. In addition, there are signed photographs of the bum and a monthly fan letter, written by the bum, in which it talks candidly to fans about life as Tony's backend.

Nowadays the bottom has its own endorsement contract with the Kruger organization (who specialize in bums) and this year there are plans for the bottom to embark on a recording career, with an album of favourite love songs entitled *The Romance of Breaking Wind* planned.

Incidentally, following Tony's revelations of his spicy love life, I was able to get hold of this compromising advert. Apparently Tony hands it out to prospective partners in any city where he is due to encamp for a tournament.

TONY KNOWLES

Full name: Anthony Peregrine Knowles
Birth sign: Donkeydong
Favourite food: Sausage
Favourite drink: A screwdriver
Favourite piece of dental equipment: Electric toothbrush with Duracells (for safe teeth)
Hobbies: Sex and water-skiing (though not simultaneously)
Favourite TV programme: Anything to do with sex or water-skiing

The Bolton Bonking Machine.

Willie Thorne

Willie's lack of hair and slightly paunchy figure have led many people to misjudge his age and assume he is older than he really is. Indeed, most people are slightly surprised to discover that Willie was in fact just thirteen on his last birthday and is the youngest player on the circuit.

One of Willie's biggest problems has been finding a suitable nickname. Last year he came close to a decision, narrowing it down to two: Willie 'Bald-Eagle' Thorne (impressive but inaccurate) or Willie 'Bald-Snooker-Player' Thorne (unimpressive but accurate). Willie 'I'm-Not-Bald-I've-Just-Got-a-Very-Very-Wide-Parting' Thorne was also dismissed. In the event, he chose neither and is still waiting for the elusive name to come along. I tried suggesting Willie 'Lend-Us-Your-Comb' Thorne at our last Matchroom Board Meeting, but he didn't seem very keen and threw a snooker ball at me.

Willie comes from that Las Vegas of the East Midlands, Leicester, which may explain why he is such a crazy, zany, fast-living type of guy.

WILLIE THORNE

Full name: William Friar Tuck Thorne
Birth sign: Vosene
Hobbies: Modelling men's bathing caps and shaving his head to allow for aerodynamical movement around the snooker table

Willie Thorne, regarded by many as the boldest snooker star on the circuit.

Kirk Stevens and Barry Hearn (Kirk is the one on the left).

Kirk Stevens

A few years ago Kirk got into hot water with a drug scandal and it seemed to destroy his chances of making it to the top. He also used to go out to night clubs and burn the candle at both ends instead of tucking himself up with a good book and a platoon of marmite soldiers, as I do. This is where so many top players seem to go wrong. What Kirk needed was sensible advice, and I was the person to give it to him.

I remember one particular occasion very well. We were staying at the Crest Hotel in Preston (my idea of a pretty wild hotel) for the UK Championships and I saw Kirk at the bar with a few dolly girls around him. Realizing he might be putting his career on the line I walked over and, separating him from the girls, I spent a good twenty minutes giving him a real earbashing and explaining why hot milk and an afternoon kip were what he needed more than anything else. Then I explained how you could get Ovaltine in a new oatmeal flavour and I handed him my jumbo-sized Steve 'Interesting' Davis thermos with the Matchroom logo on the side, telling him I'd made enough for two large mugfuls plus a little bit extra for a top up, and I urged him to retire to his room at once with the thermos and the latest issue of *Snooker Scene*.

Curiously I haven't had a chance to speak to Kirk since that meeting (every time we appear at the same function Kirk mysteriously disappears underneath a table just as I walk over to him), but I'm sure he heeded my advice.

Steven Hendry

I can see an awful lot of me in Steven: he's young, talented and made a big impact on the snooker scene very quickly, *and* he hasn't got a nickname! That's just the way I was.

I was fortunate, though, I found my nickname and everything worked out fine. But Steven might not be so lucky...He could reach twenty-six without a nickname and it could finish him off. I know it could have done that with me.

I can see the scenario now, before my very eyes. He's twenty-six, nicknameless, wonders whether the right name will ever come along and, in his panic, chooses the first name that's offered; it could be terrible – 'Fishcake', 'Pimple', 'Cheese-Sandwich', 'Abattoir', 'Sanitary Fitment'. But because of the pressure that's on him to 'get a name' he makes a rash decision and goes with the name.

After that the press are on his back: 'Hendry's New Nickname a Sham!' 'Golden Boy Loses His Touch Over Nickname!' 'Hendry's Nickname Folly Could Cost Him His Career!'

He tries to change nicknames, but the rot has set in. The strain of trying to find a new one and fight off the press ruins his game and he is finished on the snooker circuit.

One of Steven's biggest problems is his spots. Of course his manager Ian Doyle has always said that at the end of the day it's what happens on the table that counts, but I do believe there is a danger Steven's pustules might take over. I have noticed that recently he has become very possessive towards his spots, and if anyone comes near he eyes them up as a potential spot-stealer. In fact, only the other day I met him at a dinner, and he started to get very edgy, and said he'd got a new one and I couldn't have it. It's sad that someone so young has become so preoccupied with pustules that he now employs a minder simply for his spots. I can only assume it is money talking. There have been rumours of a *Join Up the Dots* TV game that Steven's face would host, plus endorsement contracts with Biactol and Spry Crisp & Dry cooking oil. My feeling is that the whole thing is probably nerves. That's why when I meet him I always try to make light of the whole thing and put him at his ease by calling out: 'Hallo, scabface, I see the spots have cleared up a bit!'

I like Steven very much and think he is a very talented player and I voice these concerns not to unsettle him but because I want to help. OK, so I could be wrong, but I've been there and back, and I know the problems he could face. That is why I now make this offer publicly to Steven from these pages come to me, talk about your problem, I will help you find a name. Natural pride and reticence may well make him cautious of voicing his concerns and making that approach, but if he values his career then I firmly believe I'm the one person to help.

So there's the offer from me, Steven, to you, Steve. Come to me and I will help you to get it right, Tadpole...

Joe Johnson

For years Joe's biggest problem was that he kept three nicknames on the go and hence suffered considerable confusion. Was he 'Ordinary Joe' (man of the people)? Or 'Gentleman Joe' (fancy shoes and dandy clothes)? Or 'Smoky Joe' (great love of curries)? Now that he has made up his mind and has settled on 'Ordinary', the future looks rosier. Incidentally, 'Ordinary' was one name I toyed with myself, but obviously it was totally unsuitable for an interesting guy like me.

JOE JOHNSON
Full name: Joe Arkthwaitethistlebottom Johnson
Birth sign: A vindaloo
Favourite food: Another vindaloo
Favourite drink: Another vindaloo and six more papadums
Hobbies: No, make that eight
Favourite TV programme: And three more lagers
Favourite holiday: Oh, and another vindaloo

NEAL FOULDS
Full name: Neal Baynton Winkham Foulds
Birth sign: Perivale
Favourite food: Mint-sauce sandwiches
Favourite drink: Double Tizer on the rocks
Hobbies: Reading the London telephone directory
Favourite TV programme: Nick Owen's *Sporting Triangles*
Favourite holiday: A week at home doing the decorating
Most embarrassing moment: Being approached for my autograph in Sainsbury's by my mum

Neal Foulds

My one criticism of Neal is that he is far too much influenced by Alex Higgins. Neal's legendary boozy late-night rave-ups and his outrageous hippy lifestyle may win over some supporters, but I for one am not a fan.

Bill Werbenuik

Last year Bill achieved a lifetime's ambition: a 147 – that wasn't a break, it was just his waist measurement. And therein lies a tale.

No matter what Bill did at the table, no matter how superb his shots, he was faced with one inescapable fact: everything was secondary to his weight. He could score three televised maximum breaks on the trot and the majority of the viewers wouldn't marvel at his snooker, they would simply nudge one another and whisper, 'My God, isn't he fat.' It is a terrible burden to bear. Bill knows that he could win the Masters ten years running and still the first thing practically everyone would say is, 'God, he's huge!' or, 'Look at him – he's so fat his thighs have different post codes!'

I'm always interested in my fellow pros' publications and this is one I found particularly interesting.

The Bill Werbenuik Health Workout Book

This is an excellent exercise for the throat muscles. The trick is regular training.

This is a particularly good exercise for the gut and stomach. Practise every day and you will soon begin to see the effect.

This exercise is very good for the arm muscles. I usually try and raise twenty or thirty pints a day like this to keep my forearm supple and in trim.

Poor Bill. What can he do? Even if he lost weight the problem wouldn't go away. Suddenly the fans would be ignoring his game again to gawp, 'Good Lord, look at Bill, what's wrong he's really lost a few pounds.' Several years on and down to a respectable weight and still, annoyingly, the problem wouldn't go away. Now the punters would watch his effortless game and say to each other over their pints, 'Of course, he's not nearly as fat as he used to be,' or, 'I can still remember when he was a real fatso.'

Really, in truth, Bill knows he can't win. And the depressing effect of this can't fail to influence his game. He'd have to keep playing till he was ninety-two before the memory of his weight was forgotten and he was released from the pressures and allowed to play his natural game. And by then, I just feel, the major titles may be beyond him.

BILL WERBENUIK
Full name: William Daisy Werbenuik
Favourite food: Food
Favourite drink: Drink
Hobbies: Taking a wingseat on a Boeing 747 and giving it a 45° list
Favourite TV programme: *The Food and Drink Programme*
Most embarrassing moment: Every day of my life

CHAPTER 12

REFEREES

Everyone naturally thinks that being a high-flying snooker referee must be just about the most interesting lifestyle around. And they'd be right. But what they forget is that it's not all wine, women and wild, wild parties. No, as a top-deck ref. like Len Ganley will explain, it all depends on training, and just like any top performer many hours of dedicated practice have to be put in each day.

Len himself, for instance, spends several hours each day locked away in a small boxroom at the back of his house adding up imaginary scores for imaginary snooker games and reciting '1 ... 8 ... 8, Eddie Charlton,' till he could practically do it in his sleep. It can be exhausting work and more than once Len has driven himself to the point of complete mental and physical exhaustion by these gruelling hours of numbing recitation.

A cream-of-the-jug ref. like John Street reckons to spend four or more hours each day on ball-cleaning practice, often picking up the same ball two to three thousand times each day, wiping it and putting it back down on its spot to achieve the level of perfection he's looking for.

You know, it's very easy for us to watch the referee at the Crucible and see only the glamour of the job as he re-spots pink and helps with the spider, but this is just the glitzy side. We forget that this ref. may have spent the last forty-eight hours without any sleep, pounding the pillow as he works out in his head over and over and over again how to say 147. Nor do we see those lonely hours locked away in his hotel room with only four walls and a video for company as he repeats, 'Foul, four Jimmy White,' silently to himself.

How to Become a Snooker Ref.

If I was asked to name the question I am asked the most about snooker, then it is almost certainly, 'How do you get to become a snooker ref.?' It's not surprising, either, because most people have at one time or another wished they could do the job. I know I certainly have!

Alas, the answer is not reassuring, because you cannot actually become a snooker ref. You have instead to be chosen.

The laws of snooker still prescribe that the snooker ref. is taken at birth from his natural mother to be brought up in complete isolation by his peers in the snooker tabernacle; an exclusive sect whose sole mission in life is turning out the generations of snooker refs. that control our game.

The novice refs. are kept apart from society and learn to devote themselves entirely to sewing the braid on dinner jackets and putting on white gloves. When they reach the age of eighteen their coming of age is marked by a bizarre initiation ceremony in which their palm is crossed thrice with snooker chalk and they sign their names in blood on the snooker stone, the symbolic high altar of the snooker priesthood. They are then sent into the outside world to referee snooker matches.

Pin-Up of the Month: Hunky Heart-throb Len 'High Thighs' Ganley.

SMASH REFS

The Len Ganley Book of Quotes

(Taken from *The Very Short Book of Snooker Refereeing Quotations*)

Here is my selection of favourite quotes from Len Ganley, appearing in this award-winning book.

'97.'
'4.'
'51.'
'37.'
'115.'
'92.'
'8.'
'16, Terry Griffiths to play, Tony Knowles and a miss.'
'42.'
'38.'
'14.'
'9.'
'73.'
'25.'
'Foul stroke four away.'
'17.'
'48.'
'13.'
'92.'
'Rex Williams has won the toss and will break.'
'Where are you going, Bill?'
'Do you want a video?'

Among those things a snooker ref. cannot do:
1. Mustn't laugh when a player misses an easy pot on a black ball finish.
2. Mustn't snort derisively throughout the match and tell the players a six-year-old could do better with his eyes closed.
3. Shouldn't stub his fag ash out on top of the white ball just as a person is about to play.
4. Must not superglue all the reds together in the triangle, 'just for a bit of a laugh'.
5. Mustn't call out the scores in a silly high-pitched whine, interspersed with violent clucking noises
6. Shouldn't walk around with a large 'Hallo Mum' sign stuck to his chest during televised contests.

CHAPTER 13

INTERESTING TIPS FOR YOUNGSTERS

One of the most interesting things you can do is play a lot of snooker. Of course it can cause quite a bit of jealousy when your friends find out that while they've been drinking or going out on dates with girls you've been raving it up on one of the tables at the local snooker hall, but that's the price you have to pay.

Here's an interesting idea for being outrageous at the school disco. Start by going up to the disc jockey and asking if he's got any experimental progressive-rock records. Then, when he puts the record on, start to dance to it in the middle of the dance floor. This should get you noticed as somebody pretty interesting immediately.

An interesting suggestion is to make a full-size snooker table during woodwork class without anyone noticing. If the teacher gets suspicious, pretend it is something else, like a houseboat, or a twelve-foot coffee table.

A final tip if you want to be really interesting is to do something totally loony, like reciting from memory the sequence of scoring shots from the previous night's snooker championships on the TV. Crazy, huh!

O Level Interestingness

1. Bob is more interesting than Tom, and Tom is more interesting than Ian. Ian is more interesting than Ken and Mike, but Derek is more interesting than Ian. Brian is less interesting than Fred and Ian, but more interesting than Derek and Tom. Who is the most interesting?

Bob
Derek
Fred
Ian
Tom
Brian
Ken
Mike
The person who thought up this question

2. Compare and contrast the toggles on a Marks and Spencer duffle-coat with one you get from Millets.

3. Describe (a) How you would apply for a subscription to *Practical Motorist* or (b) How you would make a cup of hot Bovril.

4. Complete the following sentence in no more than 4,000 words: 'Did I ever tell you about the time I…'

5. Politics. Either (a) Describe the influence John Selwyn Gummer has had on the contemporary political scene in Britain, or (b) Don't bother.

6. Using only a compass and ruler construct either Nick Owen or Jack Karnhem.

Practical

1. Make a full-size model of the Taj Mahal using old toilet-roll tubes (3 hours).

2. Watch a freshly painted wall dry.

Interesting Things to Collect as a Youngster

One of the main things a youngster does is collect things. Here are a few suggestions.

Bubble gum cards. Usually these come as a set and the idea is to collect a full set. Swaps are used to build up your set. Why not be different? Why not collect a full set of identical ones? Select a particular card and collect only this one. Stop when you have 500 and start on a new card.

Dinky Wheel Clamps. Buy enough toy wheel clamps for all your toy cars and as soon as you get up in the morning go around clamping them. Spend all day waiting for someone to come round and release your cars so you can play with them. Then, just before you go to bed, take all the clamps off again. Repeat every day.

Action Man (Conscientious Objector). Action Men are a bit passé by now. So why not ring the changes? Start by announcing to your friends that your Action Man has decided to make a stand and is joining a peace convoy. Make him a hippy shirt and a kaftan and paint a wispy beard on his face. Make a little wire fence out of chicken wire and chain your Action Man to it and leave him there for several days as a protest against an imaginary American missile base. As an alternative, give him a 'No to Nukes' placard and march him round and round in a little circle for several hours, singing, *Give Peace a Chance*.

Toy Farms. Toy farms can be rather dull. There's nothing much to do, really, other than get them out, then put them away again. Here's a tip to spice things up a bit: pretend your farm has been hit by a foot-and-mouth epidemic and all your livestock have been affected. You will have to destroy them, so pop upstairs to the loo and flush them all down the toilet. Done that? Good, right, now sit around doing nothing for the rest of the day while you wait for the government loss-assessors to come round. The end.

Another Anecdote about Alex

This final story about Alex shows the other side of the man, the side that few of us ever see, a caring side.

This incident will stay in my memory as the time Alex saved my life. It was after a tournament victory in which I had beaten Alex 9–0. I was just leaving the snooker hall when three men set upon me and started to beat me up. As I was lying there with the boots flying and punches raining down on me, Alex came round the corner and said, 'That should be enough, lads.'

If Alex hadn't intervened like that I might not be here today and I wouldn't be able to say, *Alex Saved My Life!*

STEVE DAVIs MBE!

Over the years I've picked up quite a few titles and awards: World Snooker Champion, World Snooker Champion, World Snooker Champion, World Snooker Champion, World Snooker Champion, World Snooker Champion, World Snooker Champion, World Snooker Champion, Sockshop's 'Sockman Of The Year' (1983–8), South Essex Subbuteo League semi-finalist (1974). So you can imagine, I'm a bit blasé where titles are concerned.

But the day I was told I was to receive an MBE was a bit special. At first I thought it was just another of Barry's nutty pranks. Like the time he went into that fish-and-chip shop and asked the owner if he'd got any chips left, and when he said yes, Barry said, 'Well, it's your own fault for cooking too many,' and ran out!

But then I spotted that the envelope had a first-class stamp on it, so it couldn't possibly be from Barry. That's when I realized it was genuine, and I don't mind telling you I very nearly choked on my Double-Ryvita-Cheese-Ham-Pickle-and-Sandwich-Spread.

Interesting things to talk about when receiving an award from the Queen

I was lucky. I could keep the Queen amused for hours with my crazy, off-the-wall snooker stories, but you might not be so fortunate. These are my top tips for investiture chat:

- The difficulty you had finding somewhere to park.
- What's coming up at the moment in your allotment.
- Your camping holiday last year in the Mendips.
- Your Frank Spencer impression.
- A graphic description of a car accident you've just witnessed.
- Last night's *Blankety Blank*.
- How milk bottles are made.
- Any sentence that begins: 'You look a lot different on the telly...'

Of course, receiving a great honour like an MBE is really the icing on the cake for me, but for you it might seem an impossibility. Think again. If you plan carefully, you can short-circuit your way to top honours.

Quick ways to get onto the honours' list:

1. Win anything at all at tennis.
2. Be a lollipop-lady for seventy-five years.
3. Sail round the world single-handed in a bathtub.

Barry and the MBE

I was a bit worried Barry would be envious of me being given an MBE, but luckily he isn't that sort of guy. He even threw a special party in my honour at the Little Chef just outside Chigwell on the A11 (special set menu, £2.75, coffee not included). Unfortunately, in his enthusiasm Barry forget to invite me to the meal, but he did bring me back a doggie-bag, so I didn't feel left out.

Computer Games

Having read all about me it probably won't shock you to know that another of my outrageous hang-ups is computer games. There is nothing I like better than to curl up with a mug of hot chocolate, a packet of Nuttal's Mintos and my latest computer game. Here's a few that have caught my fancy.

World Librarian. You are in charge of a municipal public lending library and have to handle the new titles accession list for the whole library. If you fail you are banished to shelving in the non-fiction section. Lots of high-power thrills.

Ninja Bicycle Repairman. Pit your wits in this intergalactic battle of nerves as you attempt to repair a faulty valve on a bicycle inner-tube and work out why the rear mudguard keeps catching. A fast action game of tactics.

International Shoveha'penny (Commodore). Vivid full-colour simulation game using powerful three-dimensional graphics. 'The most authentic shoveha'penny computer game yet … very realistic' (*Computer Games Monthly*).

Ninja Terry and June. You are June Whitfield. You have to negotiate Terry's boss arriving, and an unexpected arrival by the neighbours, a visit from the vicar, six strange Japanese business colleagues of Terry who drop by for tea, the sudden disappearance of Terry's underwear and a case of mistaken identity with someone you thought was the man Terry was trying to hide from but was in fact a completely different person called in to fix your friend Beatie's cooker. All without making one single funny joke.

Masters of the Romford and District Bus Timetable. You are cast as a medieval knight, drawn in battle against the six other knights of the land. Only one knight may win and claim rights to the kingdom. You are asked to choose weapons and you choose knowledge of the Romford and District bus timetable.

The Amstrad Ken Barlow. You are Ken Barlow and must sub-edit the classified pages of the *Wetherfield Recorder* before going off to fetch Tracy from school at quarter to four because Deirdre is busy on council business. (Approximate length of game, twenty-seven hours.)

The Future

As a sci-fi buff I am naturally interested not just in other worlds, but in our own world of the future. And I'm prepared to go on record now and say that it is my firm belief that before long we will be able to travel forward in time.

But what would this mean?

One of the most important repercussions would be in snooker, for we would be able to travel forward and see the result of any game or contest we took part in. We would be able to see whether we won or lost and therefore we would be able to withdraw from any game we were about to lose before it actually took place.

Of course, the effects of this could be quite unnerving. Everyone bar the final winner would drop out of a tournament before it began, leaving that one player to play the entire contest on his own. So many withdrawals

would take place that victory would simply depend on a player turning up.

Another advantage of time travel is that it will allow things to quicken up. For instance, now when I play 8-Eddie Charlton that game may take several hours. But in the future I will be able to travel forward in time and cut out the bits where he hops round the table checking on the lie of the balls, and reduce the game down to eight minutes.

Outer Space

One of my special hobbies is sci-fi. There's nothing I like better than to curl up in 'Steve's Den' with a milk-chocolate digestive and a 5,000-page science-fiction novel.

And as a sci-fi freak you won't be surprised to learn that, yes, I do believe there is an alternative life force out there. But what? Well, no little green men though, that's for the amateurs.

My Theories

Here are the four theories that in my mind command the greatest respect.

1. The Negative Doppelgänger Theory. This theory states that for every world there is an equal and opposite world. Thus there is another humanoid world out there that is the complete reverse of our own in every detail. A world where a fat, boring Steve Davis is bottom of the world rankings. True? Maybe.

2. The Superior Intelligence Life-Force Theory. This states that the galaxy and intelligence expand to infinity. Thus there is a world out there with intelligence infinitely more superior to our own. A world where everyone can achieve a maximum 147 break the first time they pick up a cue. A world where no shot is ever missed and TV commentators actually predict shots correctly. Possibly true.

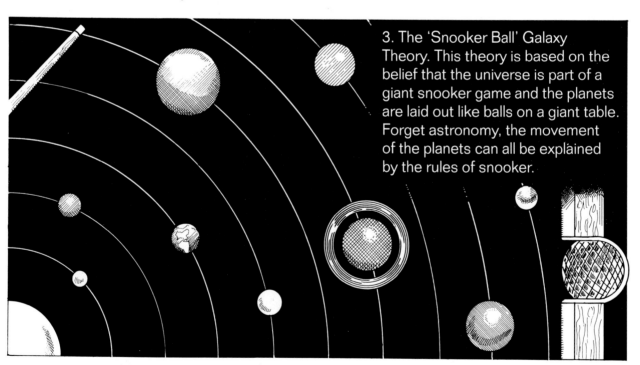

3. The 'Snooker Ball' Galaxy Theory. This theory is based on the belief that the universe is part of a giant snooker game and the planets are laid out like balls on a giant table. Forget astronomy, the movement of the planets can all be explained by the rules of snooker.

4. The Planet 'Snookus' Theory. This fourth and final theory lays claim to the belief that there is a world out there which exists for no other purpose than snooker, and where existence is a bit like watching BBC2 all day during the week of a big tournament.

Dan Dare

Many people struggle to decide what one thing they would take with them to the desert island on *Desert Island Discs* (my idea of a pretty crazy programme!). I don't, I know instantly what it would be: my collection of *Eagle Annuals*.

With these around, who needs company! I've always been a big Dan Dare fan and secretly often dream that I am in his boots.

Here is probably my favourite ever Dan Dare story from a rare 1958 edition of the annual. I hope it gives you as much enjoyment as it has given me!

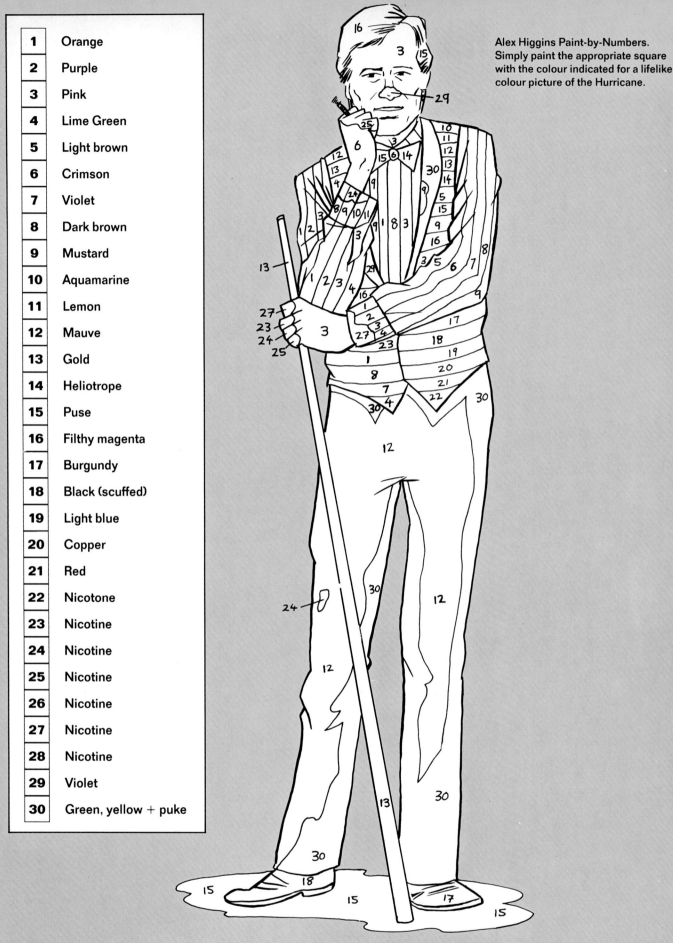

1	Orange
2	Purple
3	Pink
4	Lime Green
5	Light brown
6	Crimson
7	Violet
8	Dark brown
9	Mustard
10	Aquamarine
11	Lemon
12	Mauve
13	Gold
14	Heliotrope
15	Puse
16	Filthy magenta
17	Burgundy
18	Black (scuffed)
19	Light blue
20	Copper
21	Red
22	Nicotone
23	Nicotine
24	Nicotine
25	Nicotine
26	Nicotine
27	Nicotine
28	Nicotine
29	Violet
30	Green, yellow + puke

Alex Higgins Paint-by-Numbers. Simply paint the appropriate square with the colour indicated for a lifelike colour picture of the Hurricane.

Colour by Numbers

Here's a chance for you to create your own 'Snooker Masterpiece'. Alex has been an artist for many years, and here's your chance to join him by colouring in this specially commissioned portrait.

LIFESTYLE EXTRA
THE STEVE DAVIS
GUIDE TO
LIFE

As someone who has enjoyed the privileged benefits of being interesting, I feel I ought to repay the debt by sharing the secrets with you. *The Steve Davis Guide to Life* is packed full of interesting information that you'll find invaluable in plotting your life ahead.

Haircuts

Being a bit of a razzle-dazzle high-wire mould-breaker, I take pride in my appearance. After all, when you're the most charismatic person in British sport you have a reputation to live up to. That's why I take a lot of trouble with my hair.

OK, so some people will say it's a pretty outrageous cut, and I guess, OK, I'd have to agree, but then that's just the sort of maverick lone-star hell-raiser I am!

Kerry from 'A Cut Above' in Romford Covered Market explains how she cuts Steve's hair

'Steve's hair is very easy to cut because he's very particular about what he wants, innhe, I mean I usually wet the hair first. Then towel dry it. Then I usually start with the story of my friend Dawn's boyfriend Gary an' how she's not sure if she wants to finish with 'im or not, like, because sometimes like he can be really, really nice to her, know what I mean, then other times he can be really horrid and nasty and mean and say really, really horrible things, what do you think, Steve, because they still love each other, then after that I usually follow on with a what-d'you-think my friend Babs should do, because she's been going out with that Terry now for three years and the relationship just doesn't seem to be going anywhere and if I were her I'd think about breaking it off, although I'm not her am I, Steve, is that hot, sorry, can you lean back a bit, that's better, then I normally add a Debbie-and-Mike-have-split-again, well, I mean, this is the fourth time, course it all started when they had that holiday in Mykonos together, is that too cold, well, Debs reckons Mike was flirting with one of the couriers and, well you know how they're always arguing, at it hammer and tongs, did that go in your eye, sorry, here let me wipe it, well, I wouldn't be surprised if they're together again next week, then if I've time I usually give it a quick me-an'-Greg-still-aren't-sure-if-we're-right-for-each-other, well, I mean, I like 'im an' all that but, well, I just don't know if we're cut out for each other, I mean, all our friends say we get on, but then they're not me, are they, 'course Greg can be a real, well, you know how he is, don't you, I mean this isn't the first time we've rowed like this, and then finally I finish off with a saw-you-on-the-telly again the other night, you were t'rific the way you stuck one over that other geezer with the moustache, I mean, everyone says it was absolutely brilliant, by the way, you've not got a girlfriend have you, only my friend Maria, well, she's not seeing anyone at the moment and I wondered, well, there's a party of us going down to Hollywoods on Atlantic Boulevard on Friday, well, it's Sharon's birthday, and I thought… Oh, you're off then? All right who's next? D'you want spray?

A Funny Story About Haircuts

Quite often people want to know why my hairstyle never changes. There is a funny story to this. The barber I normally visit has a number of photos of top cuts on the wall, and alongside these is a small mirror, although to begin with I didn't know it was a mirror. I would regularly go in there, see my reflection in the mirror, not realize that was what it was, and say, 'I'll have one like that, please.' This went on for about five years, until the barber stopped me one day and said, you do realize that is a mirror you're pointing at? How we laughed. I don't mind telling you that, rollerball, devil-may-care guy that I am, I still felt a proper charlie.

Luckily the barber was able to help and pinned up a photo of me alongside the other shots. Now when I go for a haircut I can just point at the picture of me and say, 'I'll have one like that, please,' and not feel a fool.

A Pretty Wild Anecdote

I remember one year I'd just won the Fidelity Championships against Cliff Thorburn and I was relaxing at the disco afterwards with a pint of Ovaltine (OAPs don't give a XXXX for anything else) when a girl came up to me and said, 'Hey, is that a blue shirt you're wearing, Steve?' and I looked round and saw that the ultraviolet lights in the disco had made my shirt look blue! So I said, 'No, actually it's the ultraviolet lights that have made it look blue, but it's really a white one, actually,' and she said, 'Oh, I see,' and walked away. Of course, looking back it's easy to laugh about it, but at the time it was a pretty tense moment for me, I don't mind telling you.

Clothing

Sometimes when I'm at the table I wear a black waistcoat and white shirt, then other times I wear something crazy and different, like a white shirt and a black waistcoat. And the still other times I'll go completely overboard and put on something madcap and outrageous, like a different black waistcoat and another white shirt. But then that's just the sort of live-for-today, crazy, rollercoaster, hip guy that I am, always dressing on the edge!

And it's not just when I'm playing that I cut a fancy dash. At home relaxing my wardrobe is just as headstrong. For instance, one day you might catch me in a black dress suit and a white shirt. Then the next day my shirt might pop a button and I'll have to step into fashion overdrive and put on another white one from the laundry cupboard.

Me modelling stepladders.

FASHION:
Me showing that the Kipper Tie can look pretty stylish if worn correctly. Another advantage with this particular tie is that it converts to a very handy sleeping-bag when not being worn.

I don't know why more men don't wear kilts. Here I am wearing one for a publicity session, and I really believe it is one of the most flattering shots ever taken of me.

A dramatic scene at a London nightspot when I am attacked by a man jealous of my jacket.

Me as Ray Reardon.

Me as Tony Knowles.

Fancy-Dress Parties

People are always coming up to me in the street and saying, 'Steve, we've got to go to a fancy-dress party and we haven't got a clue what to wear. Have you got any interesting suggestions?' Luckily, I can help out. 'Take a tip out of my book,' I tell them. 'Do what I do and go as a top snooker player!' I do it every time I'm invited to a fancy-dress party and I haven't been stumped yet.

Me as Cliff Thorburn.

Me as Terry Griffiths.

Me as Rex Williams.

Me as Bill Werbenuik.

Me as Alex Higgins.

Me as Jimmy White.

Me as Kevin Parker (Essex Junior Under- 21 Champion, 1973–4).

Me as the Matchroom Team.

BOW-TIES

Even really top pros don't realize the rich pickings that bow-ties offer them. I do! Zany, devil-may-care tricks with the bow-tie are my stock in trade. You won't wonder why people call me the craziest guy around when you hear these stunts I get up to with mine.

The Bow-Tie Slightly Askew

How's this for starters. I put my bow-tie on normally at the start, but halfway through the session I re-adjust it so it's slightly askew. Usually no one notices until the end, when I let it be known that my bow-tie's been askew for the last two hours. To really get the press corps' notebooks out I repeat the trick in the next session, altering the bow-tie halfway through so it's askew the other way. Hard to believe, but trust me, it's true.

The Bow-Tie the Wrong Way Round

You may have thought the 'askew trick' was completely OTT, but it's small fry compared to this next trick. Before the session I actually fasten my bow-tie the wrong way round, then I wait for someone to spot my deliberate mistake. This can really liven up the sitting and waiting part of the game to a fever pitch.

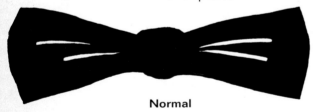

Normal

Bow-tie wrong way round

Bow-Tie Turned Round the Wrong Way

But my *pièce de résistance*, and what a riot it is too, is to emerge with the entire bow-tie turned round back to front before the session. Even I can't top this trick. And I bet you can't either!

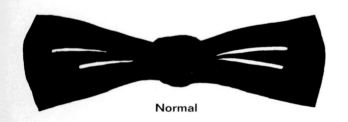

Normal

Turned 180°

The Joy of Socks

One of the things that marks me out from other men is my extensive sock wardrobe. Indeed, so great is my sock consumption that the local Sock Shop has opened a trade counter especially for me. I now own over 2,000 pairs of plain black cotton socks, one of the largest private collections of socks of this type in the country.

I suppose it was this collection that inspired my interest in sockiology: the scientific study of socks. For centuries we have studied palms, crystal balls, tea leaves and goodness knows what else in our search to untangle the mysteries of man. Now it seems the secret key may be nearer at hand (or rather, foot, geddit?) in the form of men's stockings.

By 'reading' a person's socks we can unravel their character and make stunning predictions into the future (hence the oft-quoted maxim, 'Show me the sock for five minutes, and I will show you the man,' *Oxford Book of Quotations,* Footwear Supplement). Many is the time I've sat here in the Matchroom with Barry, going through each other's socks, and you'd be staggered by some of the things I've discovered.

In fact, one of the first things that Barry looks at when taking new players aboard is their socks. Poor Cliff Thorburn, I really think he was quite alarmed when he met Barry for the first time and was asked to remove his socks and place them on the desk, where Barry then examined them under a microscope.

Many of you reading this book may well feel inspired from these few words to take up the science of 'sockism' for yourselves. If you do, then a few prudent words may be in order. Always ask permission before investigating a person's socks, especially if they're being worn at the time.

There is nothing more embarrassing than trying to remove another person's shoes in a public place only to be discovered in the act and be asked to explain your actions. And I should know better than most, because this misfortune afflicted me when I first became interested in socks.

I was enjoying a quick drink in the bar of the Reading Ranade Inn after my third-round match in the Rothmans with Kirk Stevens some years ago, when who should walk in but Dennis Taylor. I'd never had a chance to inspect the Taylor foot garments before, and was anxious to take a closer look. Unfortunately, I barely knew him at the time and he was accompanied by guests.

Luckily, though, the rest of the bar was pretty quiet, and there was an excellent selection of low coffee tables that would afford me a perfectly camouflaged passage right to Dennis's feet. Deciding to act at once, I slid down from my seat and started to crawl toward my pedical objective: viz., the feet.

Looking back, I can see it was foolish bravura not to think out my plan more fully and not to spot that the tables were glass-topped, giving Dennis's party a perfect vision of my less than secretive crawl across the room on all fours. Alas, as it was, I was oblivious to the stares that greeted my journey and had spent a full five minutes at work on Dennis's feet, trying to undo his laces and remove his shoes undetected, before I felt eyes burning down on my back. Making some lame excuse about a lost Cheese Twiglet, I stumbled hastily away and left, red-cheeked and shamefaced.

Luckily, since that day Dennis and I have become firm friends and Dennis allows me to look at his socks whenever I feel the urge coming upon me, but the experience has taught me that I should always respect the privacy of people's socks and ask first.

Life in the Fast Lane

By now I bet you're probably thinking I'm some pretty crazy guy when it comes to clothes, but I still haven't told you my wildest secret! Guess what it is? No? OK, I'll tell you: I wear coloured vests. I know, incredible to believe, isn't it, but believe me, it's true! Sometimes it's a red one. And sometimes it's a blue one. And sometimes it's a Damart long-sleeved thermal one!! No wonder they call me the crazy man of Fashion Avenue!

Steve's Racy Fashion Tips

Here are my tips for the future. These are my bets for the hottest gear to get into for the coming year.

● Designer-label underpants (especially if the label is M&S)

● Hush Puppy brothel-creepers with Velcro straps (crazy fashion, crazy fun)

● Animal-feet slippers (the undiscovered fashion fad of the future, get in now and be a trend-setter)

● Moon boots (a hit in the seventies, due for a revival)

● The balaclava (a cert., the balaclava has slipped through the fashion designers' net so often that it must be due for a major craze soon, if it hasn't already started!)

A Dedicated Follower of Fashion, Steve Models the Latest Line from Hush Puppy

Hair by Amanda at 'Curl Up & Dye', 37 The Crescent, Basildon (£2.50, wash and perm)

Clothes: Model's Own

Shoes by Hush Puppies

Focus on Nick!
Name: Nick Owen
Full name: Nick Owen
Nickname: Nick Owen
Hobbies: Being Nick Owen
Likes: Being Nick Owen
Dislikes: Being called Elton Welsby
Favourite Pop Group: Nick Owen (There isn't actually a pop group called Nick Owen, but who's splitting hairs?)
Favourite holiday: Nick Owen
Favourite food: Nick Owen
Nick Owen: Nick Owen
Nick Owen: Nick Owen
Nick Owen: Nick Owen
Nick Owen: Nick Owen
Nick Owen: Nick Owen
Nick Owen: Nick Owen
Nick Owen: Nick Owen
Nick: Nick
Nick: Nick
Nick: Nick
N: N
N: N
n: n
n: n
:
:

Some of Nick's amazing achievements:
● Passing his cycle proficiency test first time.
● Being in charge of the school rabbits during the holidays.
● Being voted the scout with the neatest kit back on his first scout long camp.
● Being school Scalextric champion three years running.
● Being the reporter who first revealed the story of the missing telephone kiosk when he worked for Television South.

The Secrets of Eternal Interestingness

There is only one man who can lay claim to the secret of eternal interestingness. And that is Nick Owen.

Nick is the high guru of interestingness, and I am totally in awe of him. I remember the day Nick sent me a letter inviting me to appear on his show, *Sporting Triangles.* That was one of the proudest moments in my life and I still keep that cherished letter in my wallet as a prized possession.

Thanks to Nick I now hold the secret of eternal interestingness in my hand, for I have been privileged to be one of the select few to attend Nick's weekend courses in Eternal Interestingness, held at his high altar of interestingness home in Penge.

I am bound by the sworn laws of secrecy never to divulge this information. But the schedule for those two days should be enough to convince you of the truths that were unfolded to me.

● **Personal introduction by Nick himself**
● **Breakfast with Nick**
● **Lunch with Nick**
● **Hot milk and afternoon nap with Nick**
● **Candlelit dinner with Nick**
● **Watch TV with Nick**
● **Seminar: 'Me on Me', hosted by Nick**
● **Hot cocoa with Nick**

No wonder I can now lay claim to the secret itself!

The Three Truths of Eternal Interestingness

I now expose for the first time ever the three truths of interestingness as revealed to me by Nick.

1. Be involved in sport at a non-participatory level (Nick Owen, Frank Bough, Des Lynam, Bob Wilson, Ron Pickering, David Vine, David Coleman).
2. Wear a lightweight V-neck pullover (Nick Owen, Frank Bough, Des Lynam, Bob Wilson, Ron Pickering, David Vine, David Coleman).
3. Be totally and utterly unflappable in any situation (Nick Owen, Frank Bough, Des Lynam, Bob Wilson, Ron Pickering, David Vine).
Follow these three truths, and you too can unlock the secret.

Food

Call me a spooked-out oddball if you will, and probably you will after this, but when it comes to flamboyant eating I leave all the other players trailing in my zany wake. I guess it's natural that as such an incredible walking funball I should really know how to throw together a pretty exotic meal, as this recipe for Marmite, cheese and bacon on toast reveals:

Beware when using the cheese grater. Here I am in a real pickle after a momentary loss of concentration with the Red Leicester

MARMITE, CHEESE AND BACON ON TOAST

1. Toast the bread. (I usually use a Kenwood six-setting adjustable-thickness pop-up toaster, although you could use the grill of a cooker if necessary.)
2. Butter the toast.
3. Put the Marmite on the toast. (Never use the same knife as you have used for the butter or you can end up with buttery bits inside the Marmite jar, which is really nasty and yukky next time you want to use it.)
4. Grate the cheese and put it on the toast.
5. Add the bacon to the toast.

Serving instructions

Serve hot with a Wagon Wheel.

I usually recommend a bottle of 'Tizer the Surpriser' with this meal, but for a real spread to remember, why not try a glass of Barbican Alcohol-Free beer?

As a special treat, you can give your sandwich that really individual touch with a set of alphabet toastie stencils. These are cra-zee!! I have one with the letter S on it, and another with the letter D, so that I can individually monogram my sandwiches with one letter on each side: DS (er, hang about, that's not quite right, is it?). To give your sandwich that racy, wildcat, state-of-the-art look, why not choose a set of different stencils from mine, to match your own initials. (Although obviously if you are called Steve Dawson then you would have the same initials as me: SD, amazing!)

SPECIAL NOTE

Several people have claimed that the STEVE DAVIS MARMITE, CHEESE AND BACON SANDWICH is a powerful aphrodisiac. I cannot substantiate these claims, although I have noted that whenever I eat one in public women seem to drift away from me, and I can only assume they are avoiding me, aware of the alluring power it might have upon them if they came too close. Be warned, you eat this sandwich at your peril!!!!!

WARNING

MY GUIDE TO SNOOKER

INTERESTING

(Reprinted from 'An Interesting Frame with Davis', first published 1985, [Matchroom University Press])

An Interesting Safety Shot

This is an interesting safety shot to play when breaking off at the start of the match.

White must be aimed against the side cushion to play a plant on black using the two reds at the foot of the triangle. Black then doubles back up the table striking blue and yellow toward the baulk cushion.

White must have sufficient backspin to cannon back into pink which dislodges brown, while white dislodges green to create a stockade around the white ball at the baulk end of the table.

If correctly played, the colours should completely surround the white ball with no possible means of escape, and secure an automatic snooker.

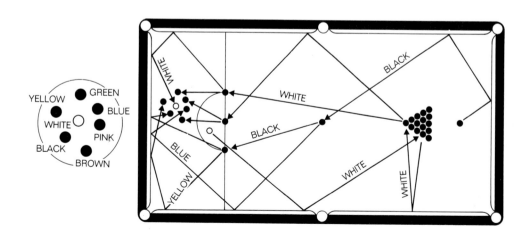

This shot is not simple, but with practice should come quite easily. (Avoid playing too often or it can become slightly predictable and boring.)

Example two.
How to marshal the red balls into a corner and build a corral of colours around them.

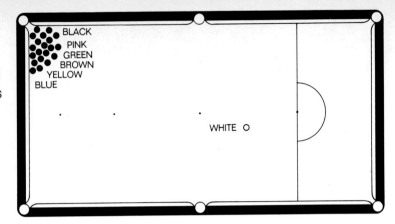

BLACK
PINK
GREEN
BROWN
YELLOW
BLUE

WHITE O

A Useful Safety Shot

Here is a useful safety shot to play when breaking off. The cue ball swerves round blue, circumnavigates the pack, kisses second from the top red without dislodging it, then makes a complete circuit round blue before finishing an S-turn around brown and green and coming to rest back in the D.

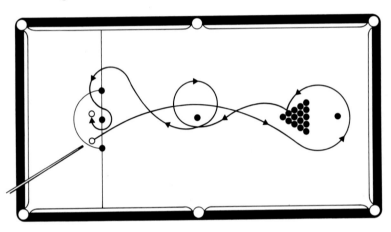

This shot serves no useful purpose, other than upset your opponent for being too defensive, but it does make sure you get used in the 'What Happened Next' round of *Question of Sport!*

Trick Shot

I strike the cue ball on to the baulk cushion, it hops off the table, pops over to the bar, pays off my slate, puts on its coat, nips off into town, picks up a pastie and a Yorkie bar for lunch, calls in at the dry cleaners to see if my shirts are ready yet, stops off at the travel agent to ask about late break holidays to Greece, checks out the prices, compares them with those offered by the other leading travel companies, goes through the holiday brochures, books a two-week half-board holiday in Mykonos for me for £299.99, pays the deposit, checks the flight times, the baggage allowances, local currency restrictions and the price of a corresponding holiday if bought at the local bucket-shop, visits Sainsbury's, picks up an individual portion chicken-and-vegetable pie for tea, shoots back home, pops the pie in the oven and sets the timer for quarter past five, tidies up, checks my telephone answering-machine, cleans the breakfast things away, Shake-'n'-Vacs the lounge carpet, makes a quick pot of tea, sits down with the paper for five minutes, pops back here to the snooker hall, takes off its coat, hangs it up, gets a round in for a couple of friends at the bar, pops out to the loo, runs a comb through its hair, shoots back to the table, leaps back on the cloth, plays a deep, reverse side screw on red into the top pocket, cannons into the pink, kisses a red and leaves itself perfectly placed for the black over centre pocket.

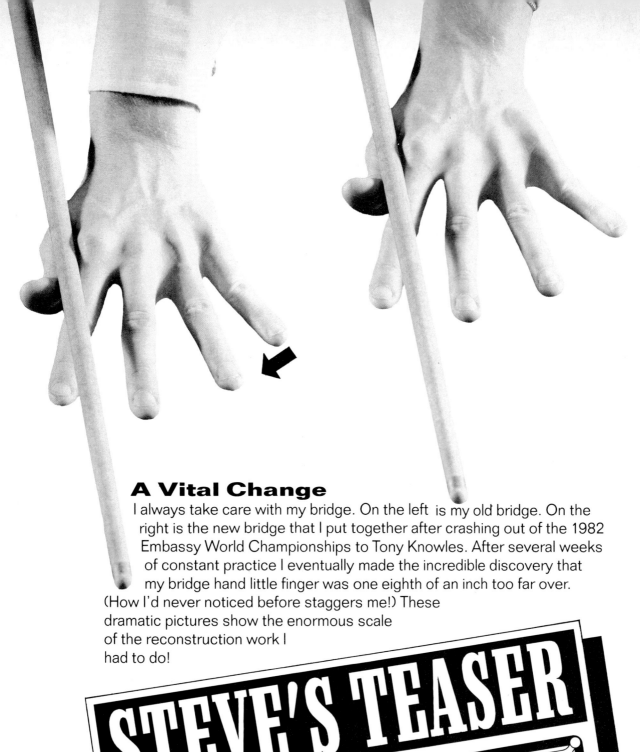

A Vital Change

I always take care with my bridge. On the left is my old bridge. On the right is the new bridge that I put together after crashing out of the 1982 Embassy World Championships to Tony Knowles. After several weeks of constant practice I eventually made the incredible discovery that my bridge hand little finger was one eighth of an inch too far over. (How I'd never noticed before staggers me!) These dramatic pictures show the enormous scale of the reconstruction work I had to do!

STEVE'S TEASER

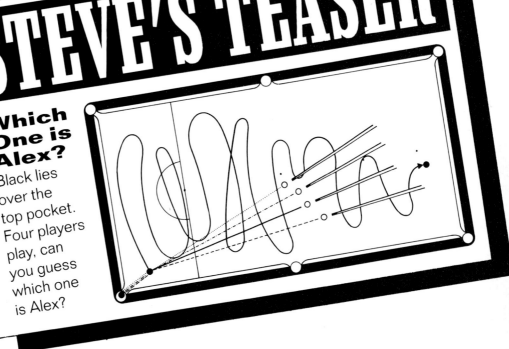

Which One is Alex?

Black lies over the top pocket. Four players play, can you guess which one is Alex?

Cliff Thorburn

This guest page was written by Cliff and shows him on the way to a break of 147 with an amazingly varied range of shots. With versatility like this, it's no surprise to learn the fans have dubbed him 'The Entertainer' and 'High Flyer'.

1. Cliff goes for an exciting screw back off the side cushion for position on black.

2. A complete change of style as Cliff uses top left-hand side topspin to sink red and get on black.

3. A long-distance stun shot gives Cliff his fifth red and again shows a vivid change of approach.

4. Cliff once again goes for the spectacular with this unusual cut back with check for the black.

5. Cliff repairs a loose guttering strip on his garage roof before re-sealing a loose fascia board using a mastic bonding-gun.

6. Cliff defies death and goes over the Niagara Falls in a barrel.

Me waiting for Bill Werbenuik to come back from the toilet to play his first shot in the opening round of the 1988 Embassy World Doubles Championship.

STEVE'S TEASER 2

You are Terry Griffiths

Here is a match situation that occurred recently. The reds are in the position shown and all the colours are on their spots except for the blue which has been knocked off its spot by a red. The table is playing fast, 5½ lengths, cloth straun, number ten (shaved), referee John Smythe. Terry trails by fifty-four points. Next shot is a red. Using your skill and judgement, try to guess which of the shots indicated were the ones sighted by Terry as possibilities.

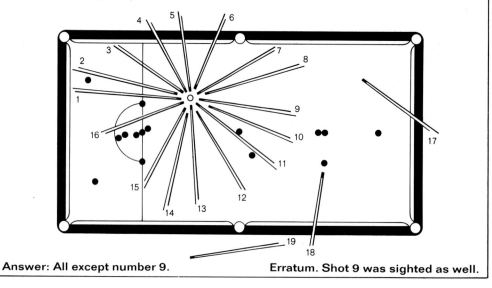

Answer: All except number 9.   Erratum. Shot 9 was sighted as well.

Who am I?

My first is in that girl off the telly.
My second is in that one in the *Sun* the other day.
My third is in that girl I picked up at the snooker hall last night.
My fourth is in that one I've been knocking off back home in Bolton.
My fifth is in that bit of foreign fluff I've been doing the business with the last couple of nights.
My sixth is that one wot was in the papers yesterday.

Who am I?

Answer: Tony Knowles

DENNIS TAYLOR'S IRISH RUBIK CUBE

This is one of Dennis's favourite puzzles: the Irish Rubik Cube. Simply take a piece of card and mark as (1). Next, fold along the edges as shown by (2) and affix the sides together with glue (3). You now have a single cube. Colour all the sides the same. Now take the cube in your hand and try to manipulate so that each side is the same colour. (Try and beat Dennis's record of two hours, twenty-five minutes.)

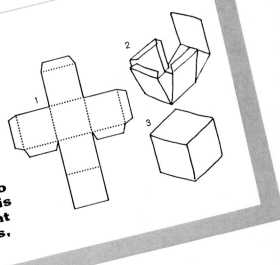

THE INTERESTING INSTANT AUTOGRAPH BOOK

No need to waste time collecting signatures with this 'instant' do-it-yourself kit. Just cut out the following world-famous names and stick them into your book for that authentic look.

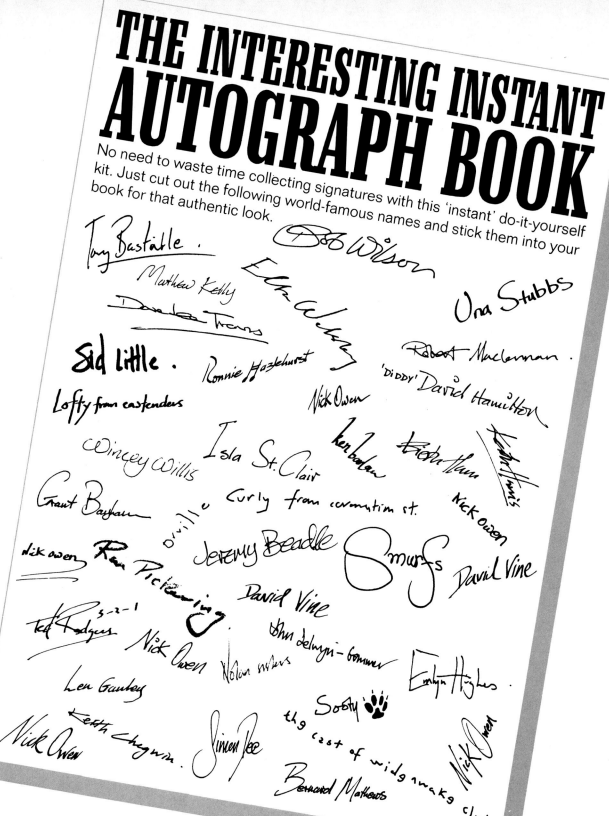

Join Up the Dots

Below you will see a number of dots. If you join up the numbers correctly you won't actually achieve anything, but it will keep you occupied while you wait for Doug Mountjoy to finish his shot.

How Interesting are You?

By now you should be getting some idea of just what an interesting, wild-as-the-wind guy I am. But what about you? How interesting are you? This simple test should help you find out!

1. You are invited to an anything-goes weekend at Hugh Hefner's place. Who do you take as your escort?

a) Your mum
b) Your wife and kids
c) Your scout troop
d) Your accountant

2. You win a million pounds on the pools and are invited to London to pick up the cheque. Who do you choose to present it to you?

a) Nick Owen
b) David Vine
c) Lofty from *EastEnders*
d) Sid Little

3. You are trapped in a lift with Jerry Hall for four hours. What do you do?

a) Try to impress her by doing your duck impressions
b) Try to get her to impress you by doing her duck impressions
c) Suggest a game of I Spy
d) Use the opportunity to go through your cheque book and add up all the cheque stubs

4. You receive a last-minute invitation to a fancy-dress party at Stringfellow's. What do you wear?

a) Your vest
b) Your Staypressed crimplene trousers
c) Your Blue Peter badge
d) Your sensible shoes

5. You decide to have a tattoo on your chest. What message do you choose?

a) I'm a Secret Lemonade Drinker
b) Radio-2: Sounds on the Easy Side
c) I Luv My Auntie Hilda
d) I am a Nolan Sisters' headbanger

HOW TO MEASURE YOUR PERFORMANCE
If you answered all the questions you are interesting. If you didn't then you're not.

STEVE DAVIS QUIZ

By now you should be getting a pretty good idea of the crazy guy I am. But how much do you really know about me? This quiz is designed to test that knowledge. Twenty statements, just answer true or false, then see how well you've done.

1. I am a world authority on Marmite Jar labels.
2. I am a former World President of the Hillman Imp Owners Association.
3. When I played Dennis Taylor in the 1985 World Final I wore a lucky 'nail through the head' trick throughout the entire match.
4. I have been married thirty-four times before and my latest wife is a Tibetan yak-farmer's daughter.
5. My favourite film ever is the Pearl & Dean cinema adverts.
6. At school I once arranged an all-night pullover party for the girls of the neighbouring sixth-form college, but only three people turned up (and two of them were my mum and dad).
7. By coincidence I have twice had to give the kiss of life to a sheep.
8. In 1984 I was approached by Keith Richards to take over as lead singer of The Rolling Stones in place of Mick Jagger, but I had to drop out because of pressure of commitments and a nasty head cold.
9. I have an autograph book made up entirely of signatures by David Vine (or 'Luncheon Voucher Man', as we know him).
10. I regularly practise at home completely nude save for a Comic Relief red nose.
11. Alex Higgins once challenged me to a drinking match and told me I could name the drink, so I chose Babycham.
12. I once played an entire snooker contest with my bow-tie slightly askew.
13. I have a time-share holiday apartment in Plumstead.
14. I once attempted to stage a school production of *The Romans in Britain* as a one-man-show.
15. I have a morbid fear of tea-strainers.
16. Barry Hearn once had a patio laid in crazy paving and I spent four days over at his place, moving the bits around, until I realized it wasn't a jigsaw puzzle.
17. I once held the British and European All-Comers Twiglet-Eating record.
18. I have been offered the main part in a Ken Russell film on three occasions and have turned him down each time because I thought it might be a bit dull.
19. I was once beaten up by the roadies at a Wombles concert.
20. All the answers given below are true.

1. True 2. True 3. True 4. True 5. True 6. True 7. True 8. True 9. True 10. True 11. True 12. True 13. True 14. True 15. True 16. True 17. True 18. True 19. True 20. False

THE INTERESTING PERSON'S YEARBOOK

Calendar of Interesting Events

Make a note in your diary of these
forthcoming interesting events.

3 Jan.	World Jigsaw International, England v Rest of World, at Trowbridge
15 Jan.	Liechtenstein motor show
28 Jan.	AGM of Ovaltine Drinkers' Association (Leatherhead)
5 Feb.	Paperclip Manufacturers' Trade Fair (Dusseldorf)
20 Feb.	The Welsh Pop Industry Awards
5 March	State visit by the Head of State of the Pitcairn Islands
17 March	Opening of new Orpington by-pass
19 March	Discuss T.K.'s latest match with him
21 March	Bulgarian Country-Dancing Championships start
12 April	Sanitary Appliances Trade Fair, Exhibition Centre, Grimsby
19 April	World Championships
23 April	Swiss Remembrance Day
18 May	Italian Fridge Manufacturers' Delegation to Britain
24 May	Start of a week of celebration to mark the twenty-fifth anniversary of the double yellow line
6 June	Display of massed milk-pudding making in honour of 200 years of the blancmange
19 Jan.	Final of the Blow Football Cup
1 July	One-man-operated buses to be introduced on the 139 route
21 July	Visit to Britain by French minister of confectionery
23 July	Lundy Island to vote on entry to Common Market
12 August	Start of British Footwear Week
25 August	Norwegian national badminton team to tour Lincolnshire
31 August	Chesterfield table-tennis league annual dinner-dance
9 Sept.	Resurfacing work on the M10 due to start
15 Sept.	Finish discussing T.K.'s latest match with him
27 Sept.	C5 owners' rally
3 Nov.	The Twenty-Fifth International Tropical Fish Show, Bromsgrove
6 Nov.	Start of the International Year of the Soapbag
19 Nov.	Save the Pilchard flag day
28 Dec.	Pope to visit Romford (to be confirmed)

THE WORLD CONFERENCE OF INTERESTING PEOPLE

to be held at
The Bexleyheath Royal British Legion
(second left outside Boots)

Life President: Sir Geoffrey Howe

Guest Speakers

The TV-am weathergirl, Frank Bruno, The Bloke from the Cold-Meat Counter at the New Tesco in Neasden, The Lead Singer from Magma, Ken Barlow, Deirdre Barlow, Tracy Barlow, Susan Barlow

MOTIONS TO BE DISCUSSED

Why is there not as much jam in doughnuts as there used to be?
Should *Tomorrow's World* be banned as subversive?
Canonization for David Vine?
The Icelandic economy
Home Rule for the Isle of Wight?
A history of fossils in the Mendip Hills
Why are some bananas more speckledy than others?
The secret sex life of stick insects
Nick Owen: A legend in his own pullover

3 June 1989

CONFEDERATION OF INTERESTING PEOPLE

Regional Offices
Anglesey, Neasden, Ipswich, Dudley,
Rhyl, Grantham, Bolton, Hull,
Keele Service Area (M6 northbound),
Minehead, Bromsgrove, Nantwich,
Dollis Hill, Wales

The Really Interesting Club of Great Britain

The Interesting Club of Great Britain (formerly The Interesting Club of Great Britain) was set up to support and encourage interestingness in people from all walks of life. Past Presidents have included Simon Dee, Peter Purvis and Joe 90.

Application is open to interesting people everywhere irrespective of race, creed, colour or hairstyle. For further details, please complete the application form below.

Name ....

Address ....

.... ROMFORD

(if different from Romford, please say why)

Maximum snooker break: ....

WPBSA world ranking: ....

Top score at snooker Scrabble: ....

Reader's Digest account number: ....

Damart thermal underwear charge-card number: ....

Favourite colour of Smartie: ....

Favourite TV newsreader: ....

Favourite drink (please tick):

☐ Ovaltine ☐ Ribena ☐ Horlicks ☐ Milk ☐ Tizer ☐ Barbican
☐ Lemsip ☐ Nesquik ☐ Kia-ora ☐ Water ☐ Bovril ☐ Cidrax

I am a crazy-as-hell person and would like to be considered for membership of the Interesting Club of Great Britain (if possible, please).

Please sign here ....

Booklist

The author would like to acknowledge the use of the following texts in compiling this work:

- The *Jimmy White Anthology of Contemporary British Literature* (previously published as *The Beano*)
- *The Jimmy White ABD of English Verse*
- *The Bible* (foreword by Barry Hearn)
- *The World Encyclopaedia of Billiard Trick Shots* by Rex Williams (new revised edition, now contains two pages)
- *The Bill Werbenuik Book of Healthy Eating* (due to be published June 2010)
- *Debretts Guide to Form and Etiquette* (Alex Higgins edition)
- *Noddy's Adventures in Preston*, by A. Higgins
- *The Reader's Digest Book of the Paperclip* (£19.50, fully illustrated)
- *Terry Griffiths: My Life and Hairstyle, an Autobiography*
- *The Good Lamppost Guide* (with a foreword by me – brilliant late night reading)
- *Nick Owen on Nick Owen*, by Nick Owen (with a foreword by Bob Wilson)